Chairs

ACANTHUS PRESS REPRINT SERIES
THE 20TH CENTURY: LANDMARKS IN DESIGN

VOLUME **3**

Chairs

edited, with an introduction by

George Nelson

with a new introduction by

Stanley Abercrombie

ACANTHUS PRESS *New York 1994*

Reprinted by:

ACANTHUS PRESS

54 WEST 21ST STREET

NEW YORK, NY 10010

212 463 0750

BOOKS@ACANTHUSPRESS.COM

1ST REPRINT EDITION, 1994

2ND PRINTING, 1999

Library of Congress Cataloging-in-Publication Data

Chairs/edited, with an introduction by George Nelson;
with a new introduction by Stanley Abercrombie.
   p. cm.– (Acanthus reprint series)
(The 20th century–landmarks in design; v. 3)
Originally published: New York: Whitney Publication,
1953, in series: Interiors library; 2.
Includes index.
ISBN 0-926494-02-3: $55.00

1. Chair design–History–20th century.
I. Nelson, George, 1908– .   II. Series
III. Series: The 20th century–landmarks in design; v. 3.
NK2715.C435   1994
749'.32'0904–dc20   93-26142
                           CIP

Printed in the USA

The Welcome Return of *Chairs*
by Stanley Abercrombie

Chairs is very Nelson. The book, like its author, is eccentric yet personable, erudite yet casual, an intellectual in corduroy, if not quite in jeans. Like George Nelson himself, it has a great deal to teach us without being for a moment pedantic.

When *Chairs* was published in 1953, George Nelson (1907-1986) was an accomplished architect-designer, internationally famous for buildings (such as the innovative 1940 New York townhouse for industrialist Sherman Fairchild), for graphics, for showroom design (including, in 1948, the first electrified track lighting), for interiors (including some for the geodesic domes of his friend Buckminster Fuller), for industrial design (the ball clock and the bubble lamp, as well as tools, kitchen appliances, and molded melamine dinnerware), for contributions to the concepts of the pedestrian shopping mall and the multimedia presentation, and for other books (most notably the best-selling *Tomorrow's House*, written with Henry Wright and published in 1945).

But Nelson was best known for his work, since 1945, as the design director of the Herman Miller furniture company. When his own first furniture collection was introduced by Miller in 1946–an 80-piece collection featuring the slat bench and modular storage components to go on it, the storage headboard, the drop-leaf desk and sectional seating–*House Beautiful* had applauded "a new pattern in furniture behavior," and *Interiors* had proclaimed "Available now: the best furniture in years!" His role as design director also allowed Nelson to bring other talent to the Miller organization, and amongst his wise selections were Charles Eames, Isamu Noguchi and Alexander Girard.

Still in the future for Nelson when *Chairs* appeared was much of the work for which he would be best known: the coconut chair of 1955, the 1959 American National Exhibition in Moscow, the sling sofa of 1963, and (with Robert Probst) the Action Office of 1964.

Prior to 1953, Nelson had also been active in fields less publicly visible, notably in teaching architecture at Columbia University and as an important force in professional design publications. This latter endeavor had begun when, after graduation from Yale, he had gone to Italy as a Fellow of the American Academy in Rome. From his base there, he sent back to *Pencil Points* magazine (later to be renamed *Progressive Architecture*) a precocious series of interviews with the European leaders of the new modernist movement, some of whom (Gio Ponti, Le Corbusier, Ludwig Mies van der Rohe) would also be represented in *Chairs*. Back in the United States in the mid-1930s, he would become associate editor, then co-managing editor (in Time, Inc. lingo, the top editorial position) at *Architectural Forum*. Beginning in 1948 he served as a contributing editor at *Interiors*; it was this last position that led to his writing *Chairs*.

Nelson's relationship with *Interiors* was complex and, in a way, serendipitous, as, in those days, his firm's office was in the same Manhattan building as the magazine's, at 18 East 50th Street. And, in addition to being a contributing editor (his name remaining on the masthead until 1968), he was also a frequent subject of *Interiors* articles, his Sidney Johnson house design in Easthampton, NY, for example, having been shown in the November, 1952, issue.

It was the right magazine with which to be aligned. Founded as *The Upholsterer* in 1934, *Interiors* had by 1952 become an enlightened advocate of modernism, far eclipsing other interior design magazines of the day in the quality of both its content and presentation. It was fortunate in its art direction, sculptor Costantino Nivola having been succeeded as art director by architect Bernard Rudofsky and then, in September of 1952, by architect Romaldo Giurgola. It was fortunate, too, in its editors: when chief editor Francis deN. "Bunny" Schroeder died in December of 1952, his place was taken by Olga Gueft, a woman of forceful enthusiasms who had been hired by Schroeder as his managing editor in 1945; Gueft would run the magazine with energy and insight for the next two decades. One sign of the vigor of *Interiors* in those days was that a section of the magazine devoted to the new profession of industrial design was developed, thanks to Nelson's urgings at the ear of publisher Charles Whitney, into a new magazine.

Industrial Design made its first independent appearance in the same year as *Chairs*, with Jane Thompson its first editor.

Chairs was the second in a series of books instituted by *Interiors* magazine to "treat all aspects of design." Whatever the original ambition may have been, only four aspects were actually treated, all four books being edited and written by Nelson and largely designed by his firm. The first, *Living Spaces*, appeared in 1952; *Chairs* and *Display* were published in 1953; *Storage* concluded the series in 1954.

"Which objects will be selected by posterity as most typical of Western culture in the first half of the twentieth century is anybody's guess, but I suspect that the contemporary chair will be somewhere on the list." So Nelson wrote in his introduction to *Chairs*, establishing both the understatement of the prose style he would employ and, beneath that casual manner, his interest in the subject.

At the time, the chair was a major instrument for the introduction of modernism, and modernism was considered a major instrument for the forging of a new postwar world of ease and democracy. Architecture was modernism's major manifestation, of course, but individuals without the funds (or nerve) to build a modern house could display their advanced taste in a few pieces of furniture. And in furniture architects or designers without clients for whole modern structures could exercise their imaginations at smaller, less expensive, less risky scale. Not that furniture served only as an architecture substitute nor that enthusiasm for it was in any way bogus. One striking thing about the furniture in Nelson's book is how good it seems today—most of it functional, inventive, practical, handsome. Not yet foreseen were the disillusion of the modernists and the dissolution of the postmodernists.

Chairs was a rather narrow undertaking, intentionally. It was not meant to be a history of modern chair design, nor was it meant to be comprehensive or didactic in any specific way. As the previous quotation showed, it limited its sights to Western culture, Nelson even indulging his opinion that "There are civilizations and races to whom the idea [of chairs] has never occurred." The project set itself no exact dates of coverage or criteria for inclusion, and its organization was by type of construction—bentwood, laminated wood and molded plastic grouped together in the first section, followed by sections on solid wood, metal and upholstered pieces. The collection of roughly 300 chairs (plus, arbitrarily, a few stools, quite a few sofas and a handful of tables) was apparently required to meet only one standard, that of Nelson's own taste.

It is interesting, therefore, to look at what Nelson included in the book and to read the nature of the collection as a barometer of the 1953 sensibility of an architect and furniture designer who was an influential figure for most of his life. However personal and unrestricted the choices, they were not the choices of a snob. Many of the examples were high style indeed, and prominent, naturally, was the work of the masters—Breuer, Aalto, Le Corbusier and Mies—but there was also much that was intended not to be specified by architects and designers (as was Nelson's own furniture for Miller) but to reach a mass market in retail furniture stores. Among these last were pieces by Finn Juhl for Baker, by T. H. Robsjohn-Gibbings for Widdicomb, by Paul McCobb for the O'Hearn and Winchendon companies and by Edward Wormley for Dunbar.

Not that popularity dominated. Nelson also selected some oddities by names little remembered today: a chaise longue by Willy and Emil Guhl of Switzerland; a wood and reed rocker by Otto Kolb, also Swiss; and exotic molded plywood designs by Vittoiano Vigano of Italy, by Karen and Ebbe Clemensen of Denmark and by "Pannaggi, Norway."

It would have been disingenuous for Nelson to exclude his own trendsetting work for Miller, and a large number of his Miller designs appeared in the book. But the greatest coverage and the highest praise went to his Miller colleague Charles Eames (typically for that time, no mention being made of his wife Ray as a collaborator). All three of Eames's important early chair designs were featured—the plywood shell chair, the plastic shell chair and the wire chair—but Nelson's most admiring remarks adhered to the first. The molded plywood design, he said, "has been given international recognition as the outstanding design of the past two decades…. no other chair has reached a comparable design level."

Not all the chairs included were praised. A chair rather awkwardly combining a seat and back of heavily carved wood with a frame of thin steel rods was described as "more interesting for the idea than for its appearance." The designer was Ettore Sottsass, Jr., who would work briefly in the Nelson office in 1957 and would become Nelson's close friend. Today it is easy to imagine the little chair's strange juxtapositions as a foretaste of Sottsass's Memphis collection still long in the future. But hindsight is misleadingly easy.

It is also interesting to consider what Nelson left out. Apparently considered insufficiently modern were the proto-modern contributions of Jean-Michel Frank, of Rietveld and Mackintosh, Horta and Gaudi, Chareau, Ruhlmann, Mallet-Stevens and Eileen Gray, even though some even earlier Thonet bentwood pieces made an appearance. Beyond the pale of consideration, one assumes, were such decorative novelties as Salvador Dali's 1936 sofa shaped like Mae West's lips, Carlo Bugatti's vaguely sadomasochistic machines for sitting and Elsie de Wolfe's little Biedermeier sidechair in lustrous Lucite. The greatest modern furniture designer omitted was undoubtedly Arne Jacobsen, but this was a matter of timing: Jacobsen's Ant chair was introduced by Fritz Hansen only in 1952, when the book was presumably already in preparation.

More surprising omissions were Gerald Summers' 1930 plywood armchair, Kem Weber's 1935 cantilevered "Airline" chair, Kaare Klint's 1933 Safari chair or his 1934 ladderback for Hansen, Jean Prouvé's 1930 steel chair for Tecta and Giuseppe Terragni's 1936 "Sant'Elia" chair for Zanotta. It is interesting to note also that Nelson apparently gave no credence to Mart Stam's claims to the first tubular steel cantilever design, giving Breuer full credit.

But, if *Chairs* was one designer's personal inventory of modern favorites, it was by no means a routine touting of modernism and functionality. With considerable experience as a practicing designer, Nelson knew better than to be doctrinaire. "We have become so accustomed," he wrote, "to assuming a link between artifice and traditional furniture, and a link between function and modern furniture, that we are often completely blind to the fact that modern designers often work for effects that have little or nothing to do with either the function or the actual manufacturing techniques of their products."

Chairs, in short, was just what it was meant to be: a personal, loosely defined and idiosyncratic sampling of great design and the not-so-great-but-interesting-anyway. Today it is a reminder not only of those thoughtful and unpretentious furniture designs but also of a whole vanished era that was looking toward the future with energetic and optimistic plans. It is very pleasant to have this book in print again.

| *Interiors* Library | 2 |

Chairs

edited, with an introduction by George Nelson

contents

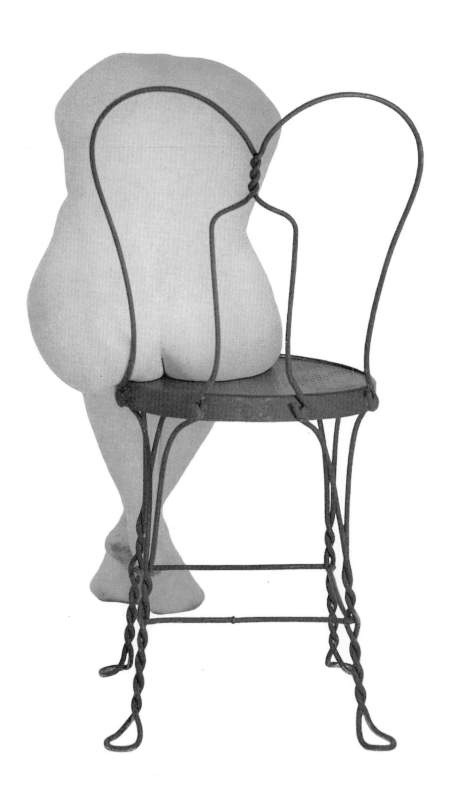

introduction

A little over two years ago the editors of *Interiors* devoted an entire issue to modern furniture, and in the course of exploring their subject, they came to the conclusion regarding seating that one could sit on almost anything—from a curb to a camel. They then went on to use the major part of the issue to demonstrate that while one *could* sit on practically anything, people rarely chose to do so, having become very discriminating in their tastes. In fact, as one leafed through the magazine it soon became evident that there exists a truly extraordinary interest in just what one does sit on, and that the trickle of new designs to which the furniture industry had long been accustomed had now grown to a veritable deluge.

It was also evident that this outpouring of ideas represented considerably more than a play for new business. Even when the designer had no client to manufacture his latest creation, he insisted on making at least one piece in his basement and he somehow got a picture of it into print. And this was not all. The greatest names in architecture since the Renaissance were to be found attached to chairs. Alvar Aalto of Finland, famed for his great sanatorium at Paimio and other buildings, found the time to design a three-legged stacking stool and a number of laminated wood chairs, and he even invented some of the techniques for making them. Le Corbusier, father of a world-wide school of building, engendered some prodigious creations in steel, leather and canvas. Mies van der Rohe designed his classic "Barcelona" chair in the course of doing an exhibition pavilion. Marcel Breuer became internationally famous for the steel chair he invented long before he made his reputation as an architect. Even Frank Lloyd Wright, who disapproves of sitting as an ungraceful and undignified posture (more and more people are coming to agree with him), has designed an impressive variety of seating pieces.

This list need not be continued indefinitely to make the two points that (a) if you design chairs, you are moving in rather fast-moving company, and (b) the chair must be a pretty important design problem to attract such an array of design talent. But why?

Every period, by some obscure process, selects certain objects to which it attaches excessive importance. The Etruscans, like other highly developed early peoples, produced grave sculptures and funerary urns in such profusion that one wonders how they ever found time to produce anything else. The Greeks spent an unconscionable amount of time on the design of coins, hand mirrors, painted vases and oil lamps. The Balinese male who does not devote most of his waking hours to carving the stone sides of temples or making decorative arrangements of fruit and vegetables is probably in a minority of the adult population. Which objects will be selected by posterity as most typical of Western culture in the first half of the 20th century is anybody's guess, but I suspect that the contemporary chair will be somewhere on the list.

To come to any idea of why the chair should occupy its currently exalted position, one has to locate it in a framework of some sort, and the framework in which the chair most frequently finds itself is the room. The room, in turn, exists only by grace of the house. And the house—at least in its most advanced forms—has changed since most of us were born, in a manner astonishing to behold. From a tightly-shuttered box it has evolved into a construction of almost alarming delicacy and fragility. Its walls have become thin posts between sheets of glass. Its wood-and-plaster partitions are dissolving into featherweight screens. Its rooms are being absorbed into spaces whose edges are hard to define, and its interior and exterior are becoming increasingly hard to disentangle.

In this rapidly developing setting for modern living, certain situations now come into being which affect the design and use of furniture. For example, we have all been taught from childhood that the place to put most of the furniture is against the wall. The manufacturers of chests and other storage units leave the backs of these cases unfinished for this reason. But when the walls disappear, the only place left for furniture is out in the open. Hence silhouette becomes important, and most traditional designs for seating become unusable. There is an easy way to test this out if you don't happen to live in a modern house. Look through the home magazines for pictures of contemporary interiors in which period furniture has been used. Invariably, when this combination turns up, the old chairs which look most at ease in their new surroundings are French provincial, Louis XV and the various kinds of Windsor chairs. What these and other successfully transplanted pieces have in common is lack of weight, relative transparency and very elegant silhouettes. These are qualities they share with the best of the contemporary designs. They are demanded by the kinds of interiors we are designing.

There is something else to be said about these interiors—they are slowly being emptied of their familiar contents, a change thoroughly documented by the volume in this series entitled "Living Spaces." At least one exterior wall is given over to plate glass, and disappears. Rugs do not seem quite as necessary as they used to be. Many portable lamps are being replaced by "architectural"—i. e. invisible—lighting. Storage cabinets have been swallowed up by the remaining walls. Sofas tend to become built-in seating. In this disappearing landscape the chair remains as one of the unassimilable objects and in consequence it becomes very conspicious. It becomes as much a piece of sculpture as an object of utility. One might now compare it to a girl in a Bikini suit, who has to pay more attention to her figure than the ladies in the bathing costumes of the Mack Sennett era. The time when one couldn't find the furniture for the decor is gone.

Thus the once-humble chair has emerged—for the time being, at least—as a thoroughly glamorous object; and I am sure that one reason it has attracted so much attention from designers is not only that it presents a problem requiring great imagination and skill, but the results are certain to attract the attention of a broad, sympathetic public. For the same reason it has become a subject of interest to the editors, and when this series was planned it seemed entirely natural to devote to the chair one of the first of the books.

I believe it safe to claim that within these pages there are assembled more contemporary designs for accommodating the posterior than one would have believed possible. And the present flood of new designs shows absolutely no sign of abating.

George Nelson

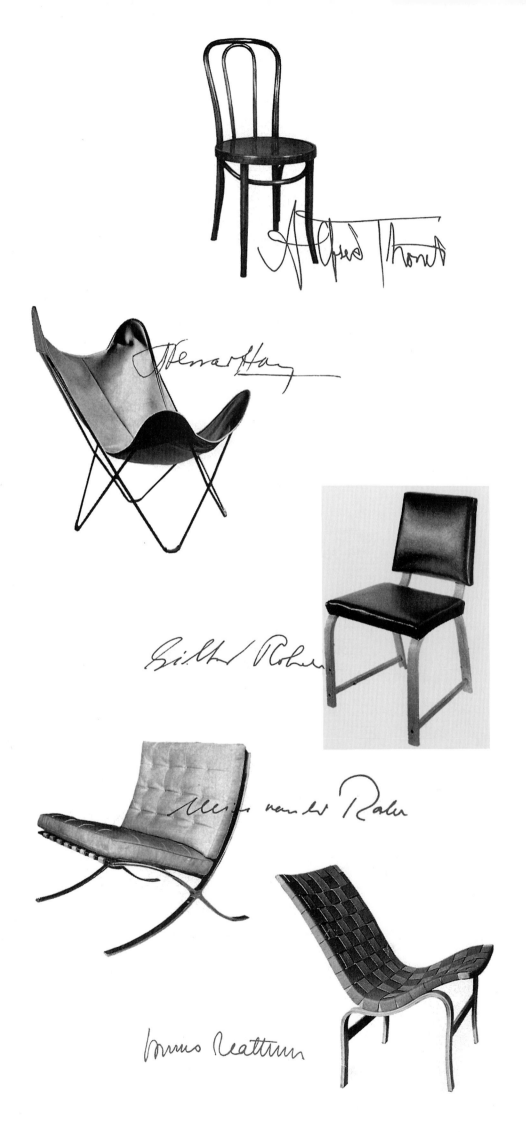

Thomas Chippendale produced countless sideboards, commodes, tables, desks, cabinets, beds, and many, many other pieces of furniture; but when you think of the Chippendale style, you don't think of the cabinet and you don't think of a sideboard. You think of a chair. It is usually of mahogany, with upholstered seat and carved open back and arms; the legs may be straight or have a cabriole curve, and the top of the back frame suggests the lines of a modified bow or a graceful pair of collar bones; it is admirably suited to comfortable sitting in an upright posture, and has an unmistakable masculine elegance. When you think of Chippendale you think of such a chair, and when you see such a chair, you think of Chippendale.

The name of Hepplewhite just as automatically suggests a chair, and—to get away from the Eighteenth Century—the same applies to Breuer, Eames, Risom, and many others who may or may not be represented by illustrations on these two pages. Today, every truly original idea—every innovation in design, every new application of materials, every technical invention for furniture—seems to find its most important expression in a chair.

Eames, for example, has employed his electronic molding and welding process in tables and cabinets, but *the* Eames piece is the Eames *chair*. Alfred Thonet could have used his marvelously strong, light, cheap, split-resisting bent rods of beechwood and his thick laminated veneers for tables and cabinets, but the Thonet product that became a standard utility in the homes, restaurants and cafes of Europe and America during the Nineteenth Century was a chair. That applies to the metal tubes that Marcel Breuer bent into springy supports and the similar spring support principle that Alvar Aalto adapted to laminated wood.

Whoever the designer, whatever his contribution, it seems always to culminate in a chair, which emerges, therefore, as a very special object of furniture. Overleaf, more about what exactly is so unique about the chair.

bentwood

sticks

tubes

stones

air

bars

Sticks and stones and tubes and bars—
these are only a few of the materials at
the chair maker's disposal. What is more,
an enormous variety of results can be obtained with any one material, as illustrated,
for example, by the three stick chairs on
the facing page. There is a huge distance,
in terms of design, between the rough hewn
bench, circa 1870, taken from a one-room
Michigan schoolhouse, and the unpretentious but well finished straight chair, and
as big a distance again between that and
the suavely angled Jens Risom product.

Where labor was plentiful, chairs were
often carved of marble, granite, or any
other stone that was handy. The two illustrated Roman chairs may not meet modern standards of comfort, but the theatre-
goers and dignitaries of antiquity found
them very impressive.

Marcel Breuer bent metal tubes into springy
chair supports; scores of other designers
have used the same material, sometimes
with similar spring action, and at other
times have bent the tubes into ordinary
legs. Aalto adapted the same principle to
curved strips of laminated wood, and Gould
and Mathsson have since employed curved
laminated strips in other designs; then we
can sit on air—provided it is surrounded
by rubber or plastic, joined by string, and
supported on sticks.

And finally we illustrate that the metal bar
lends itself with impartiality both to stark
simplicity and tortuous convolutions in
chair design.

The chair is unique among all objects of furniture in that it substitutes for the action of certain muscles to hold the body in a position other than supine. There are civilizations and races to whom the idea has never occurred. We as a people have come to believe that a chair can reduce wear and tear on spine, neck, arms, legs, and even eyes.

For each posture there are a proper angle and depth of the chair seat, back, and arms. Thus, to a limited extent, function determines the profile of the chair irrespective of its style and period. The drawings indicate the gradual alterations in chair profile as function varies from working through dining and reading to the last stage of relaxation. Note that as the sitter approaches perfect comfort, the designer's problem disappears, for, perfectly relaxed, the sitter finally transfers herself to a mattress on which she can lie perfectly straight. The Barwa chair (below) goes the mattress one better, for it permits the sitter to rest with her feet higher than her head; a position warmly recommended by physicians and beauticians.

Chair by Bartolucci-Waldheim
for Barwa Sales

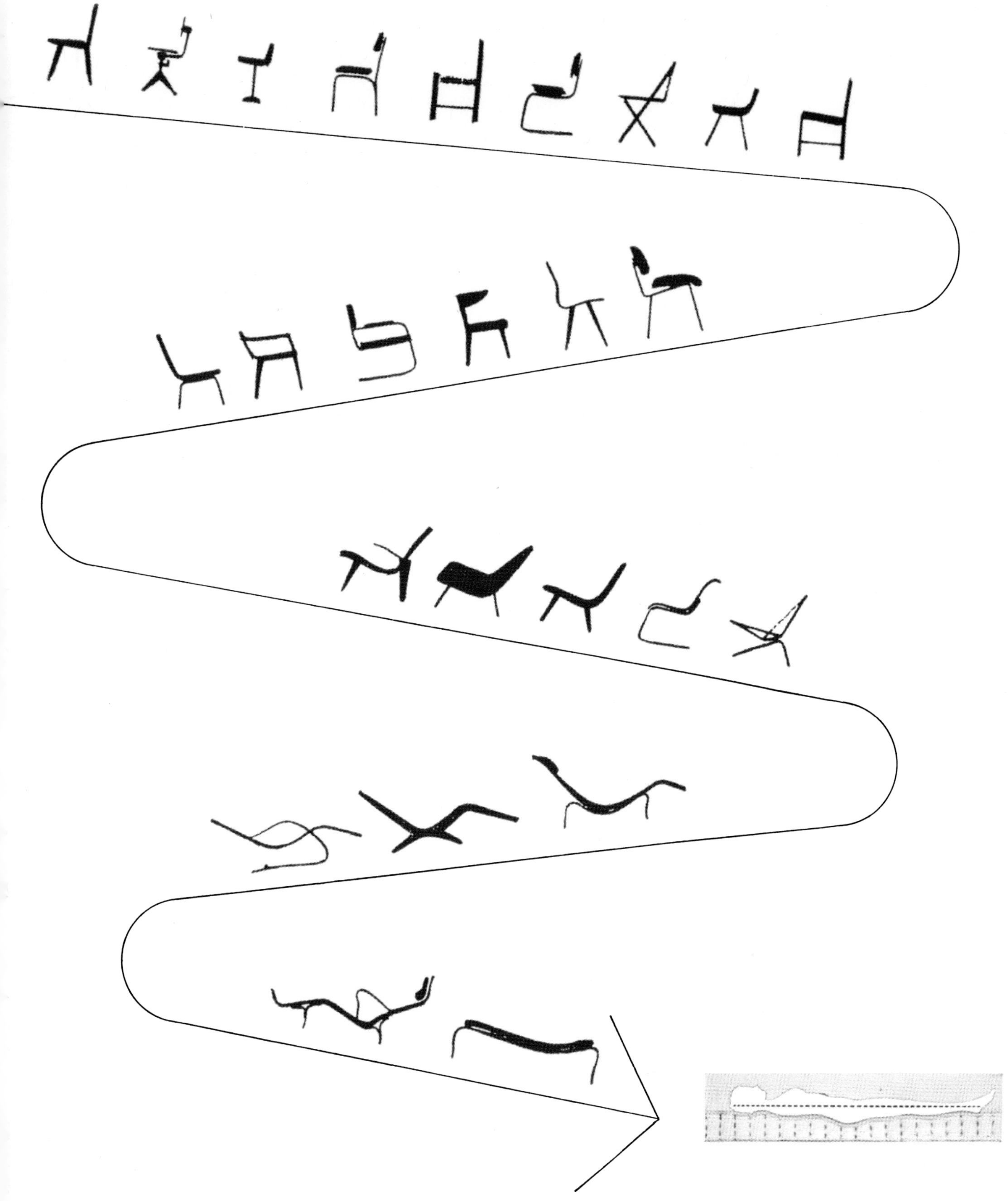

*unsupported foam rubber
on a laminated bentwood frame.
Harvey Probber, designer.*

material — its influence is twofold: 1. tactile

In solving the peculiar problem of the chair—developing a surface that feels comfortable in direct contact with the human body—designers have found a tremendous range of technical solutions in many kinds of material, yielding and unyielding, soft and hard. Each material implies a certain type of structure. Some are illustrated in the drawings. Others might have been included such as foam rubber upholstery, flat springs, and air cushions; not to mention any number of combinations: springs combined with loose cushions of down or foam rubber, and webbing combined with the same.

Time was when we could say that unyielding materials could be assigned automatically to work chairs, and yielding materials to chairs for relaxation. Because of technical advances in shaping unyielding materials, this is no longer true. The modern electronic molding process brings the old carved slab back in line with today's technology.

solid wood

stamped metal (tractor seat)

molded wood

reed or straw

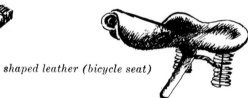

shaped leather (bicycle seat)

flat upholstery

webbing

deep springs

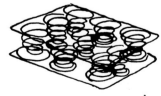

foam rubber laminated to wood

loose cushions, down or foam rubber

Windsor chair

Robsjohn-Gibbings design, Widdicomb Furniture Company

Nakashima design, Knoll Associates

Alden B. Dow design, custom

Alf Sture, Norway

Edward Stone design, The Bartos Company

2. material as structure: wood

For the great mass of furniture made today, we use exactly the same material that has dominated the field for thousands of years—wood—and we put it together in virtually the same way as has been done for hundreds of years. This material and structure permit a certain degree of freedom in design, but also impose certain limitations. That is the reason for the resemblence among all the chairs shown on these two pages—not only the obvious similarity between the antique Windsor and the modern Nakashima, but the others also. Where manufacturers have deviated from traditional methods of construction (not of finishing or ornamenting) there has been a frequent loss of quality in their products. Thus technical changes have affected the low-cost, high-speed mass market rather than the quality furniture field. There are still few substitutes for mortices, tenons, and glued joints in wooden furniture.

Marcel Breuer design, Thonet Industries, Inc.

material as structure: metal

When Marcel Breuer developed his tubular steel chair 26 years ago, he dramatically demonstrated a fact that had been hinted at by Thonet's bentwood chair and the old-fashioned ice-cream parlor chair; namely, that the mainspring of progress in the *technique* of manufacturing furniture lies in bringing new materials into the field. Breuer's achievement was twofold: first he used a new material; and second he applied a new design principle to the chair by substituting a double "S"-shaped support for the conventional four legs. This move eliminated many joints; gave the chair comfortable resiliency at low cost. Soon the idea was applied to other metals beside steel; later new principles were added, such as the suspension in the Hardoy chair.

Baldwin-Machado design

Hardoy, Bonet, Kurchan designers, Knoll Associates

Swiss design

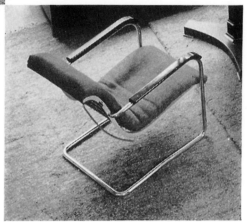

*Van Keppel-Green
designers and manufacturers*

*Andre Dupré design,
Knoll Associates*

*George Nelson design,
Herman Miller Furniture Company*

Alvar Aalto design, Finsven

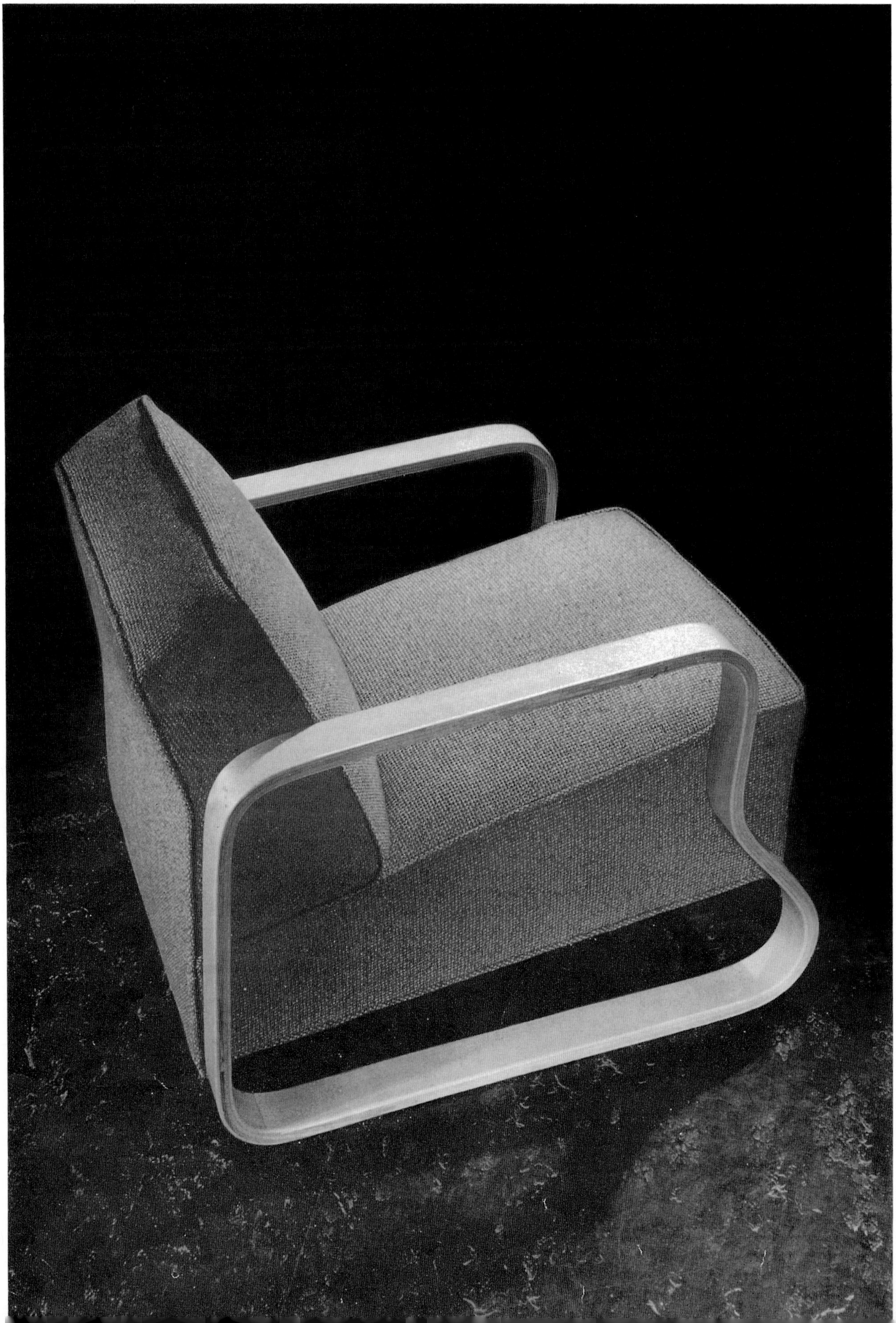

Alvar Aalto design, Finsven

Eero Saarinen design, Knoll Associates

material as structure: laminations

Many remarkable inventions had been invented, and many remarkable materials had materialized, long before anyone realized that they could be brought into the parlor. In his *Mechanization Takes Command*, Siegfried Giedion traces the patent for lightweight, strong, springy, economical bent laminated plywood to the time of the Civil War. It had been in common use for decades for the seats in trains and trolley cars when Aalto applied it to modern furniture design. The Mathsson chair at left incorporates still another basic innovation—the separation of chassis from the legs, which has, among other advantages, that of compact stacking for economical shipping and storage.

Bruno Mathsson design, Bonniers

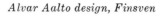

Alvar Aalto design, Finsven

material as both a structural and tactile medium

Speaking of the probable future of modern furniture, the Eames chair is a significant signpost towards it—not so much because of what it is, but because of the combination of new principles that Charles Eames incorporated in the design. He not only used new materials in new ways for their structural and tactile qualities, but also created a form with a distinctive visual and artistic personality. Eames applied many recent developments in hard seating: information on how to mold plywood, information about comfortable pos-

ture and body contours. He attained resiliency in his hard seat by two means: a frame using the springiness of both tubular metal and laminated wood; rubber shock mounts electronically welded to the wood and steel by a process independently and almost simultaneously invented by two Italians, Cristiani and Fratino. (page 32)

But what sets the Eames chair apart is that it is a total design package, integrating new techniques with modern art forms into a unified design that, perhaps more than any other, symbolizes "Modern Furniture."

Hardoy, Bonet and Kurchan design, Knoll Associates

Hardoy design, custom

Aalto design, Finsven

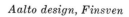

Albini design, Knoll Associates   *Nelson design, Herman Miller Furniture Company*

Mies van der Rohe design, custom

The form of a chair (or any other piece of furniture) is dictated by many factors—material, function and esthetics. Nevertheless, the form may demonstrate a life of its own, an initiating force, an inherent validity that makes it capable of adaptation to media other than the one in which it was originally presented. Long after the material of a certain chair may have become obsolete, or outdated, or may simply have ceased to be available, its form may continue to be repeated again and again in other materials.

As designers use certain forms interchangeably in many materials, these forms become part of a common fund of designs. Actually, most of them always were; since very old, their original designers are unknown. Each of the three pairs of illustrations on these two pages are well known examples of this adaptation process. The principle of suspension in a rigid cradle is retained in both the metal and wooden Hardoy chairs. The wooden version, which folded, was used by Italian officers in North Africa before Hardoy found it. Where *they* got it we don't know. The other two pairs of designs require no explanation. In each case the structural principle lent itself admirably to more than one material.

Mobile, Alexander Calder

Eero Saarinen design, Knoll Associates

Carlo Mollino design, custom

Charles Eames design,
Herman Miller
Furniture Company

Bases of Eames chairs,
Herman Miller Furniture Company

The foregoing pages have emphasized the role of materials and structure in chair design. There is another factor, hard to isolate but very important, which is suggested by the examples shown here. It has to do with the designer's sense of form, which, of course, is also a period sense of form shared by the painters and sculptors as well. To some extent it can be shown that the work of modern artists has directly influenced the designers, but in most instances it would be more precise to say that both had been similarly conditioned. In the Mollino chair one senses the designer's pleasure in the contrast of wirey lines and heavy shapes, something also to be found in Miro's paintings, but one does not necessarily stem from the other. The similarity between the Eames chair frames and the wire constructions of Calder is another case in point.

Fontana-Radici design, custom

Florence Knoll design, Knoll Associates

Savoye house, Le Corbusier and Jeanneret, architects

two movements in design

The furniture designer is not only a worker in materials, a solver of technical problems, but also an artist and psychologist. As such he tends today to produce designs that fall into one of two diametrically opposed types—the shocking, and the soothing.

The first, illustrated above by a Maurice Martiné chair, exploits the techniques of stimulation. The eye is excited by opposing masses and erratic movement. There is violence in the comparison between the light wire frame and bold, sharp seat and back forms, between

open areas and bulky masses. Acute bends and sharp angles force the eye to change direction abruptly. The Mathsson chair on this page, though just as up-to-the-minute in visual quality and far ahead of it in manufacturing technique, aims at an effect that has more generally been applied to traditional forms and methods of manufacture. Instead of contrast, it exploits harmony. Seat, back and legs form a unified composition that the eye follows without conscious effort.

three design influences: 1. the handicraft look

The more one examines furniture design, the more one is impressed with the importance of psychological factors, as opposed to technological ones. We have become so
accustomed to assuming a link between artifice and traditional furniture, and a link
between function and modern furniture, that we are often completely blind to the fact
that modern designers often work for effects that have little or nothing to do with
either the function or the actual manufacturing technique of their products.

At this point it is necessary to point out that although many effects in furniture design have been criticized as phony, not all effects are necessarily dishonest. As a
matter of fact, we have illustrated three predominating influences—or effects or
"looks" on these pages which seem important today. The three looks are: 1. the
handicraft look; 2. the machine look; 3. the bio-morphic look. Each of these effects
was used to emphasize a facet of living which the designer liked or felt was needed.
The handicraft look, illustrated here, has nothing to do with whether the chairs were
made by hand or not; the Finn Juhl pieces were, but the others incorporate a number
of machine operations. But when that easy, rounded look that spells home and comfort was achieved with machines, it was nevertheless achieved without straining either
the machine or the method.

Tapiovaara design,
Knoll Associates Inc.

Elias Svedberg design, Nordiska Kompaniet

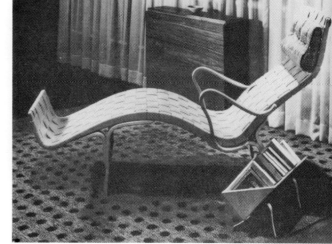

Mathsson design, Bonniers and Baldwin-Kingrey

Finn Juhl design, Carl Brorup

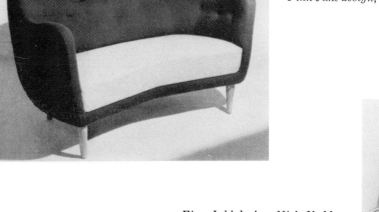

Finn Juhl design, Niels Vodder

Alf Sture design

2. the machine look

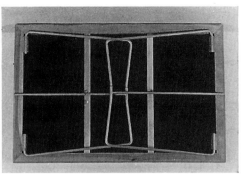

*Eames table, Herman Miller
Furniture Company*

*William Armbruster design,
Edgewood Furniture Company*

Cristiani and Fratino design, custom

Odelberg-Olsen design, Knoll Associates

Cristiani and Fratino design, custom

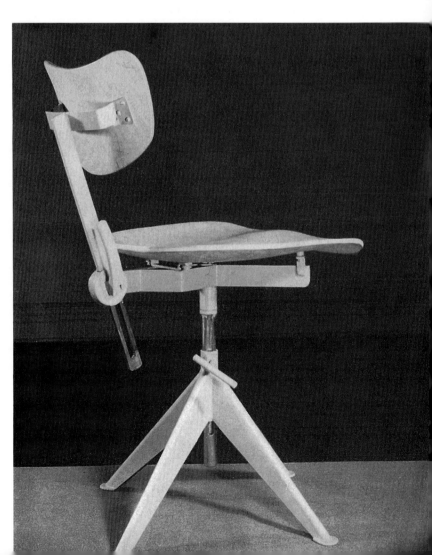

3. the biomorphic look

On the preceding pages, were illustrated cases in which designers used machine methods to attain a hand-crafted look. On the facing page are cases in which designers used either hand or machine manufacture to achieve a machine look. The object was not to deceive anyone that the hand-made object was made by machine—as if that were any virtue—but rather to dramatize machine forms and emphasize the role of the machine in modern life. In the Eames and Cristiani-Fratino furniture, the machine look is appropriate in that these are true products of machine technology. Nevertheless, since the same methods of manufacture could have been used to produce more rounded, less angular, less machine-like forms, the machine look must be considered contrived in these pieces too. In the Swedish swivel chair and glass table the machine look is entirely of the designer's devising, for these are hand made objects. Finally, some designers have striven to dramatize what we may call the bio-morphic, biological or organic form—neither homey like the handicraft object nor rigid like the machine form—but amorphous and flowing like living tissue. This is the style of sculptor Isamu Noguchi who has designed both hand and machine made furniture. It is his pieces that are illustrated on this page.

Isamu Noguchi designs, Herman Miller Furniture Company

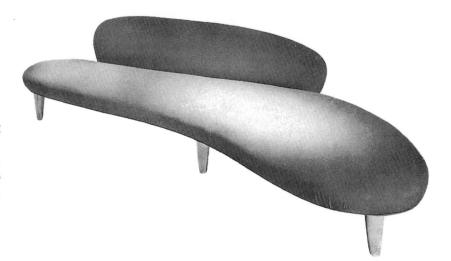

Note on organization of material: In a field as complex as seating has become, a great variety of possible arrangements of material suggest themselves. One could, for instance, group the illustrations on the basis of material, of processes and of functions; but no one seems entirely satisfactory since in each instance overlaps are unavoidable. The choice made here was to arrange the examples primarily on the basis of processes and materials used in manufacture. Thus the reader will find a section devoted to seating pieces in which solid wood is the major material and another in which metal plays the most important role. Where forming or molding as a process takes precedence over the materials, this classification has been attempted. It is hoped that this arrangement will prove workable for the majority of readers. No apology is made for the overlapping of categories since in all cases this appears to be inevitable.—ed.

bentwood

laminated wood

molded plastic

Alvar Aalto, at the age of 54, is one of the world's great architects and designers. His tuberculosis sanatorium at Paimio in Finland has been internationally admired for two decades and was one of the first large-scale structures to demonstrate convincingly the validity of the contemporary approach to architectural design. The first Aalto chair was designed in 1932 and followed the lead of designers in Germany; within three years, however, he had developed his own unique approach to furniture, using a native material—Finnish birch—and the technique of laminating and molding thin layers of veneer. These designs, many of which have shown no need for change in almost twenty years, stand out as one of the major technical and esthetic achievements in this field and, taken by themselves, would have been sufficient to establish the reputation of a lesser man. There are two factories making Aalto furniture today, one in Finland and another in Sweden. Most of the pieces, new as well as old, can be obtained in the U. S.; Finsven, importer.

One of the truly classic designs in bentwood is shown above as a side chair and the variation with arms. It is made of beech and cane, and the modern version is a slight adaptation of the original design by Joseph Frank. Knoll Associates, importers.

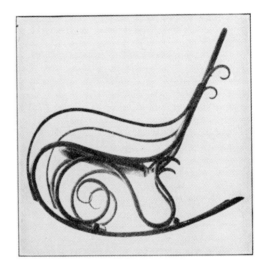

The use of bentwood is a relatively old technique for making furniture, and the name of Thonet has been associated with it for about a century. At one period, before World War I, its complex of European factories was producing as many as 18,000 chairs a day. Early models (above) were executed in the florid taste of the period, but appearance should not be allowed to obscure the fact that many of these chairs were soundly engineered to give a combination of great strength and light weight. One of the recent designs produced by the U. S. company has a bentwood frame and removable covers and is part of a group of sturdy and economical institutional pieces. Thonet Industries, Inc.

A stacking armchair of Finnish origin. Seats and backs are of molded plywood. The upholstered versions have foam rubber padding. Ilmari Tapiovaara, designer. Knoll Associates, importers.

Chairs with laminated frames and supports. They can be used as sectional seating units. Manufactured in caned, webbed and upholstered versions. Pascoe.

An unusual variation on the theme of the folding chair, executed in laminated maple. Seat is padded with foam rubber. Pascoe.

An armchair which is given added resilience through the use of a hairpin curve in laminated maple. Pascoe.

One of the early Aalto designs. Birch plywood has been bent to form a one-piece back and seat. Finsven, importer.

Somewhat like the Morris chair in its adjustability, this armchair has upholstered foam rubber cushions set on supports of wood and cane. The frame is a continuous construction of bentwood. Edward Wormley, designer. Dunbar Furniture Corporation of Indiana.

A very personal and successful approach to the possibilities of laminated wood. The cantilevered seat structure is stiffened by the stretched leather. Allan Gould, for Allan Gould Designs.

A very involved design executed entirely in bent and molded plywood. The supporting frame is doubled for strength—something which would be hard to achieve with any other wood technique. Note the complete articulation of all parts: support, seat, back and headrest. The designer, Hans J. Wegner, is best known for his beautiful adaptations of tradtional chair designs. Johannes Hansen, cabinet maker.

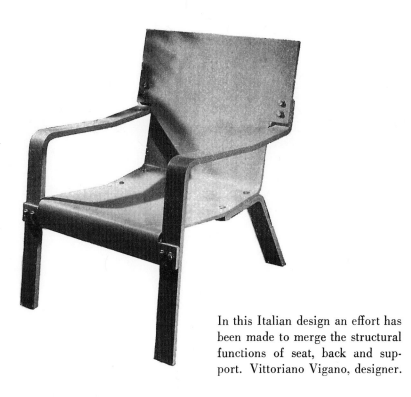

In this Italian design an effort has been made to merge the structural functions of seat, back and support. Vittoriano Vigano, designer.

Stacking chairs from Denmark, in both side and armchair versions. Peter Hvidt and O. Molgaard Nielsen designers for Fritz Hansen, Copenhagen. Hansen, importer.

Chairs constructed on the snowshoe principle, using bent ash and laced transparent rawhide, have been made for years and have enjoyed a certain popularity in the cabin type of vacation place. These two chairs represent an attempt to arrive at a more contemporary form, and hence wider acceptance. Designed by Carl Koch, for Vermont Tubbs, Inc.

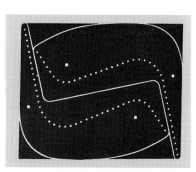

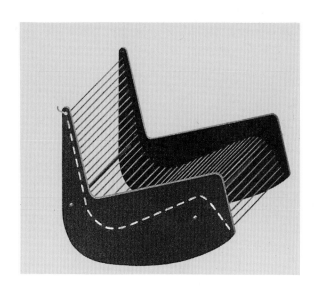

A design not currently in production, but interesting in its approach. It was awarded a third prize in the Museum of Modern Art-sponsored competition for low-cost furniture. The chair consists of two flat sides of plywood, two struts to hold them apart and a combined seat and back made of cord in tension. Diagram above shows how sides can be cut with only a small waste of material. Alexey Brodovitch, designer.

Several versions of a Swiss architect's ideas for a low-cost rocking chair. The illustration above shows a combination of laminated wood and woven reed. The others illustrate the same structural idea, but use spaced strips of canvas as the supporting material. The center photograph (left) has the rocker set in a fixed frame to make an armchair with several seating positions. The furniture was photographed at the architect's own house in Switzerland. Otto Kolb, designer.

 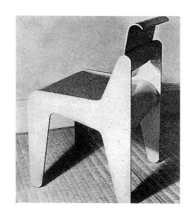

One of the most important names in the history of contemporary furniture is that of Marcel Breuer. While a student at the famed Bauhaus in Germany (1920-24), he executed a number of interesting projects in furniture, and in 1925 he invented the tubular steel chair, of which countless millions have been produced. In review of this particular development, it might be remarked that in all the subsequent variations there has been no basic improvement on the original Breuer designs.

Laminated wood is a material which has continued to occupy a great deal of Breuer's attention, and it has generally been his preference to use it as shown here: not bent, but cut out of sheets of plywood. Some early experiments, carried on between 1934 and 1939, are shown in the illustrations at the top of the page. More recent examples are the armchairs in open wood slats and upholstery. All of these are designed for minimum waste in cutting and easy assembly.

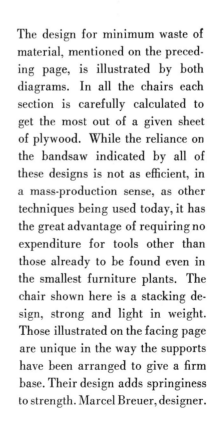

The design for minimum waste of material, mentioned on the preceding page, is illustrated by both diagrams. In all the chairs each section is carefully calculated to get the most out of a given sheet of plywood. While the reliance on the bandsaw indicated by all of these designs is not as efficient, in a mass-production sense, as other techniques being used today, it has the great advantage of requiring no expenditure for tools other than those already to be found even in the smallest furniture plants. The chair shown here is a stacking design, strong and light in weight. Those illustrated on the facing page are unique in the way the supports have been arranged to give a firm base. Their design adds springiness to strength. Marcel Breuer, designer.

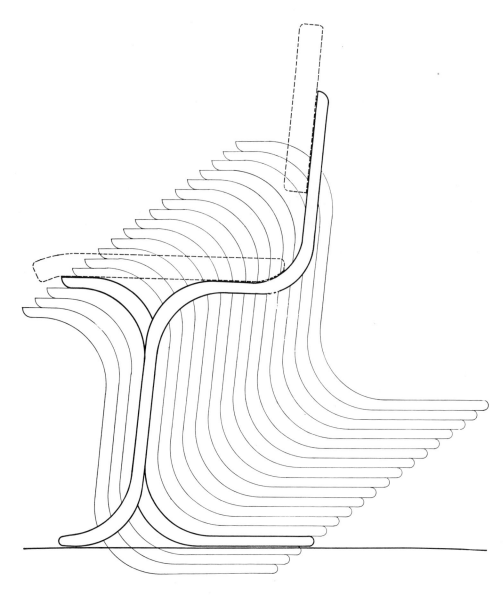

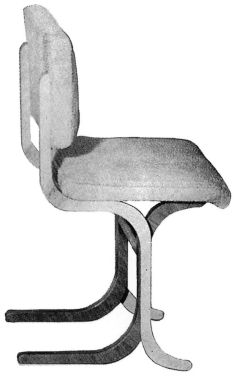

Dining room furniture designed for the Hotell Malmen in Stockholm. Made of laminated red beech, the chair frames and arms consist of only two components. A padded backrest acts as a stiffener, linking seat and back rail. While simple in construction and attractive in appearance, the chairs meet the requirements of hotel use in a completely satisfactory way. They were designed by architect Carl-Axel Acking, who was responsible for the design of hotel interiors and furniture.

These chairs are of exceptional technical interest. Side frames and arms, for example, are molded from one piece of laminated wood. The design was worked out for knockdown shipping but shows none of the appearance characteristics of this type of furniture. Hvidt-Nielsen, designers. Manufacturer: Fritz Hansen, Denmark. Herman Miller Furniture Co., importer.

An extreme example of the combination of carved and molded components. Birthe and Torsten Johansson, designers; A. J. Johansson, cabinet maker, Denmark.

A desk chair in mahogany and black leather, very typical in shape and finish of best Scandinavian custom work. Jacob Kjaer, designer and cabinet maker, Denmark.

From the day it was first shown, the Eames chair has been given international recognition as the outstanding design of the past two decades. There is good reason for its reputation, for no other chair has reached a comparable design level, whatever the basis for evaluation. Technically, the design is impeccable. Two pads of molded plywood are fastened to wood or metal frames with rubber shock mounts as the connectors. The result is a seating device which is comfortable, resilient and close to indestructible. The design works in terms of mass-production techniques, as demonstrated by the fact that there now exists a factory set up entirely for its production, using tools of an advanced type. Esthetically the chair is a completely integrated expression of form, function and manufacture. Charles Eames, designer. Herman Miller Furniture Co.

A side chair with a one-piece molded plywood seat and back. This formed piece is connected to a metal base by three bolts. Designer: Karl Lightfoot, for Lightfoot Studio.

This Italian design is quite similar in principle to the example above although the form in which the idea was realized is very different. Carlo Mollino, designer.

An interesting variation on children's schoolroom furniture. The chairs consist of separate seats and backs of bent birch, attached to frames of cast metal. Designer: James Leonard, England. The furniture was imported by Knoll Associates.

The backs of these chairs represent a translation of an old design, once executed in solid wood, into a new form made possible by today's laminating and bending techniques. Each back is a solid piece of plywood, cut out, bent and inserted into the seat with tabs, as in paper box construction. Borge Mogensen, designer; Erhard Rasmussen, cabinet maker, Denmark.

Bent plywood shells, supported in front by themselves; at the back, by a single metal rod. Produced in France.

The "compass" chair, a strong, simple design in which seating and structural requirements have been fused. Designer: Allan Gould, for Allan Gould Designs.

With the rapid development of plastics, it was inevitable that designers would turn to molded shells. The chairs above, prize winners in the international low-cost furniture competition of the Museum of Modern Art, were originally presented as stampings of mild steel coated with neoprene but finally produced in a fiberglass-reinforced polyester. Charles Eames, designer. Herman Miller Furniture Co.

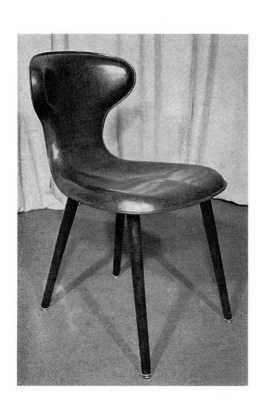

An entry in the competition mentioned on the opposite page, the result of research at the Armour Research Foundation. An award was given for the report by James Prestini and Robert Lewis on the use of resin-impregnated wood fiber. This experimental lounge chair was conceived as a molding, with seat, back, arms and legs designed for production in a single unit. The chair was designed by Brenner, Speyer and Prestini.

A molded side chair of reinforced plastic, designed to be furnished either plain or with a resin-impregnated fabric fused to the surface. The designer reports that a 500-ton press can mold a unit every eight minutes. Designer: Egmont Arens, for the General American Transportation Company.

A plastic shell with a glued-on plastic connector for the metal supporting frame. It is offered in six colors. The piece is lightweight, resistant to flame, water and stains. Designer: Hobart Wells, for Lensol Wells.

These stools are of composite construction. The seats are of molded plastic bolted to leg supports of bentwood. A chair of similar design and construction is also available. Thonet.

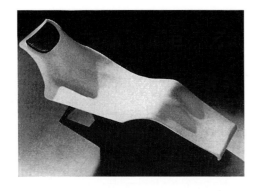

Two entries in the low-cost furniture competition mentioned earlier. Above, a one-piece design in molded plywood. Designer: Pannaggi, Norway. Left, a form-fitting reclining piece by Willy and Emil Guhl of Switzerland.

An armchair shown at a recent exhibition of the Swiss Werkbund in Zurich. The slung seat and back, of woven reed, is held in a frame with carved arms. Designer: Willy Guhl.

One of the best designs in bent plywood which can be used either as a desk or lounge chair depending on the type of base selected. Ray Komai, for the J. G. Furniture Co.

An upholstered model, with foam rubber and fabric on a plastic shell. The chair is also made with an upholstered seat and exposed back in black plastic. Designer: Eero Saarinen, for Knoll Associates.

A very personal expression of the molded shell theme, obviously not calculated for large-scale production. Karen and Ebbe Clemensen, Denmark.

One of the more successful of recent British designs. The chair follows a pattern familiar in contemporary design: rod supports for an upholstered seat, but deviates in the use of a special arm-and-back unit in bent plywood. Lounge and side chair versions are shown. Designer: Robin Day, for S. Hille and Company. John Stuart Inc., distributor.

Largest of the plastic shells in production, this is a true lounge chair with high back, separate cushions and broad arms. A metal cradle supports the shell. Designer: Eero Saarinen, for Knoll Associates.

An articulated version of the same general type of seating as the example above. Separating the chair into two units introduces the possibility of greater resilience and somewhat reduces the initial tooling problems. Designer: Alvin Lustig, for Paramount Furniture Co.

A reclining piece consisting of a foam rubber slab on a platform. Legs are a combination of solid and laminated wood—a type of construction often seen in Scandinavian furniture. Designer: Edward Wormley, for Dunbar Furniture.

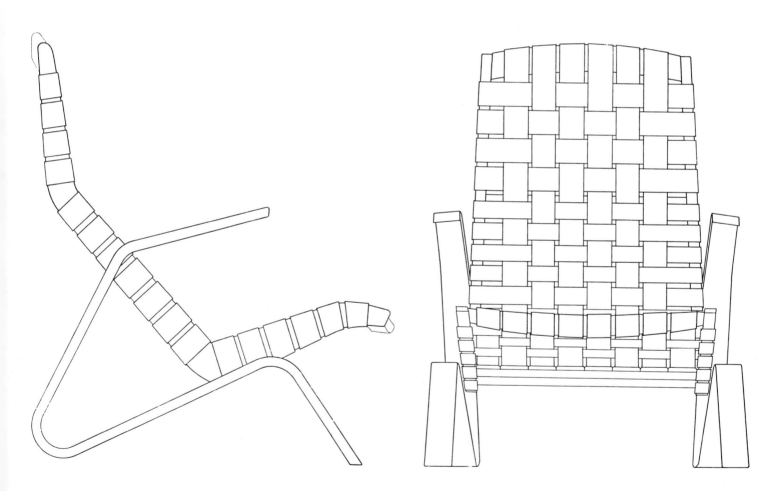

A lounge chair in laminated birch, with a solid wood frame. The combination arm and support has been very ingeniously contrived to make a firm base and rigid connection with the frame. The chair is shown here with its webbed covering (photo opposite). It is also available fully upholstered. Designer: Eero Saarinen for Knoll Associates.

A chaise, halfway between the flat reclining platform such as the piece opposite, and the fully contoured type. With its thin cushion and gracefully curved frame the piece has unusual elegance. Designer: Edward Wormley, for Dunbar Furniture Corporation of Indiana.

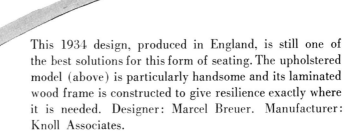

This 1934 design, produced in England, is still one of the best solutions for this form of seating. The upholstered model (above) is particularly handsome and its laminated wood frame is constructed to give resilience exactly where it is needed. Designer: Marcel Breuer. Manufacturer: Knoll Associates.

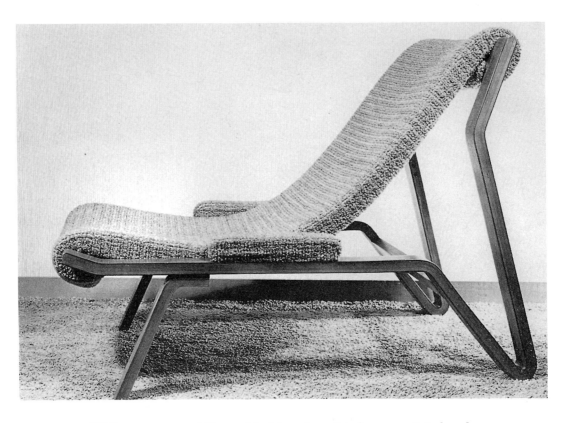

While not an especially good-looking piece, this lounge unit is based on an exceedingly interesting idea. A sandwich of two-inch foam rubber and canvas, covered with upholstery fabric is fastened to a rigid stretcher at the front and to a resilient back frame. The result is remarkable comfort. Designed by Harvey Probber in cooperation with the Hewitt Restfoam Company.

The laminated wood furniture of Karl Bruno Mathsson occupies a unique position, and it has been in a process of continual development for about twenty years. The forms have steadily become more refined, the pieces more elegant and the structures have become lighter. It would be instructive to compare this example with the model shown in the introduction (page 21). Importers: Bonniers, New York; Baldwin-Kingrey, Chicago.

Only a contemporary Italian would concoct as complicated a group of adjustable units. The basic piece is an armchair (left) which can be tilted back as shown below. An auxiliary piece is the footstool, whose front legs can be folded back when it is hooked on to the chair to make a chaise. Designers: Rita Bravi and Luisa Castiglioni, Italy.

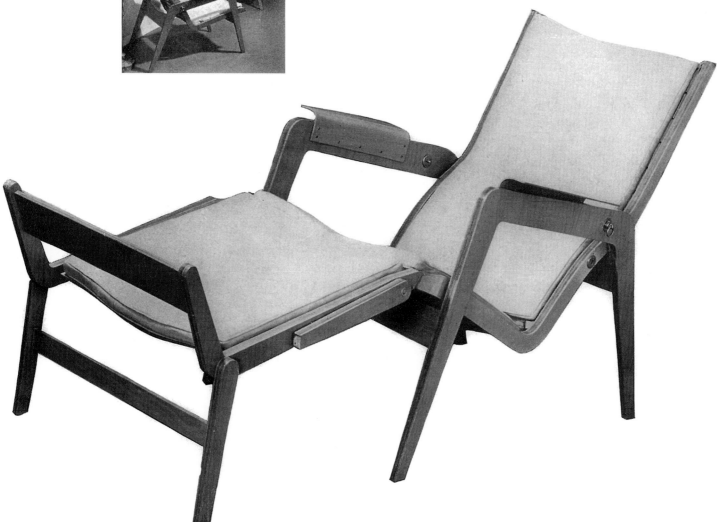

solid wood

A very primitive-looking chair, designed for the efficient utilization of standard lumber stock. John Sheehan, designer and manufacturer.

Appropriately described as a "sun fan" chair, this comfortable-looking piece recalls handmade prototypes but was designed for machine production. The frame is constructed of shaped solid wood; the "fan" back is composed of birch rods. Sonna Rosen, designer; Swedish Modern, importer.

Ezra Stoller

Walnut dining chairs, with seats of woven hemp, as used in an apartment by architects Reisner and Urbahn. George Nakashima, designer and manufacturer.

The illustration above shows the use of authentic originals of the Windsor type in a house of contemporary design by Eliot Noyes. This "mixing" of styles, so often a source of confusion to the layman, is indulged in with considerable frequency by modern architects and designers.

Fran Byrne

"Pin chair"—a new version of a traditional Swedish handicraft design. To judge from the shapes and construction, this model must follow the original rather closely, much more than the Rosen design on the opposite page. Bengt Akerblom, designer; Swedish Modern, importer.

This bench was part of an interior design project (a lounge in Keio University) carried out by the sculptor Isamu Noguchi in Japan. Although there is an obvious connection with early wood designs, Noguchi's personal touch is very much in evidence.

A space-saving chair with a quarter-round seat. Four of these chairs nest in a circle under a 36-inch diameter table. Gilbert M. Garte, designer and manufacturer; George Mason Inc., distributor.

A modern version of a traditional officer's sword chair, designed to be useful in cramped quarters. Here the original was clearly used for the idea but not the forms. Designer: Carlo Mollino, Italy.

Contemporary designers, in much the same way as the modern painters and sculptors, show a strong interest in the primitive and frequently let themselves be influenced by forms developed centuries ago. The seating pieces on this page offer examples of this tendency, and their interest depends largely on the nature of the designer's creative response, since there is always the possibility that the new piece may turn out to be little more than a period reproduction. Generally speaking, the best modern furniture of the past dozen years shows a less direct preoccupation with the forms of primitive prototypes.

A knock-down chair in birch and cowhide by one of the best contemporary Finnish designers. The seat can be adjusted to three positions. The chair is one of a group of three designed by Ilmari Tapiovaara for Thonet Industries, Inc.

This saddle stool can be set up in two heights, depending upon the pattern of the seat. It is the same in construction as the traditional artist's folding stool. Two finishes are available for both tripod base and leather seat: natural and black. Designer: Don Knorr, for Kneedler-Fauchère.

Formal low-backed armchairs in maple, birch or cherry. Sole leather straps in their natural russet color are used for both seat and back. Stewart Ross James, designer; Hansen, distributor.

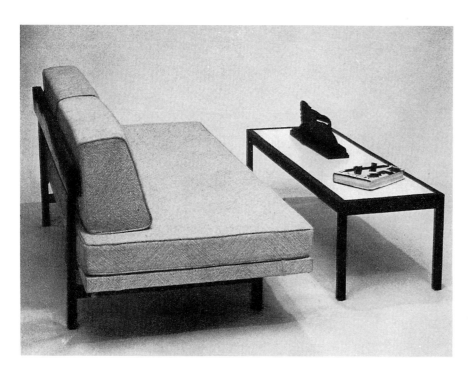

A platform couch which serves as a bed when the loose back bolsters are removed. This type of unit has become very common and is being used to replace the earlier type of day bed. Allan Gould, for Allan Gould Designs.

This "loom chair" takes its name from the interlacing of seat and back webbing. The chair is adjustable. Elenhank Designers.

A new version of the officer's chair. It is made of oak bound in rattan or rawhide and has removable seat and back covers. The chair is manufactured in Japan for the McGuire Company of San Francisco. Eleanor Forbes, designer.

A set of light, delicately detailed dining chairs in cane. The foam rubber seat pads can be snapped on and off. Designer: Edward Wormley, for the Dunbar Furniture Corporation of Indiana.

Above, a new version of the Adirondack chair in walnut. The table arm is optional. Below, spindlebacked chairs in walnut with upholstered seats. There is a matching armchair (not shown). These are also Wormley designs for Dunbar.

Both of the chairs above have the hand-crafted look so commonly seen in Scandinavian furniture, but they were designed for factory production. Examination of their parts shows that the seemingly involved shapes lend themselves easily to manufacture with the standard woodworking tools. The materials are teak and beech, with rush or cord for the seats. P. Olsen Sibast, designer. Swedish Modern, distributor.

An early chair in wood by the Italian architect whose current designs in wrought iron, reed and rattan (see page 106) are being produced by the John B. Salterini Company. Designer: Maurizio Tempestini.

These are two models of a chair which has been produced in Italy in several variations over a period of years. The basic structure is always the traditional framework illustrated, in which the back legs also form the back. Characteristic features of this chair are the pointed legs and the inclined back support. It is a particularly interesting example of the many variations possible within a limited range. A third version, not shown, is being currently imported. Gio Ponti, designer; M. Singer & Sons, importers.

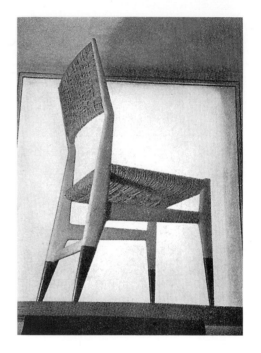

These two chairs offer another illustration of variations within a theme. The dining chair has an upholstered slip seat which is interchangeable with caned or webbed frames. Harold Bartos designer, for Lehigh Furniture Company.

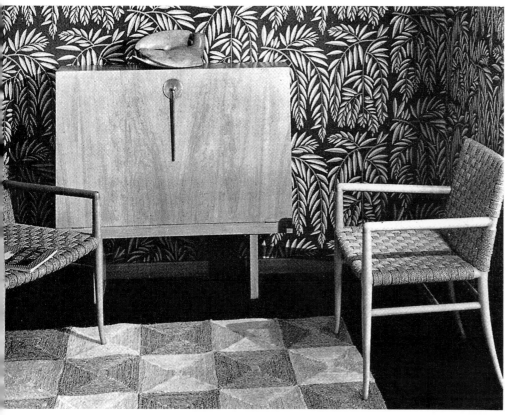

All of the furniture shown on these pages forms part of the collection designed by T. H. Robsjohn-Gibbings. It is one of the best-known groups in the country and has had an influence on furniture trends. An outstanding characteristic of all the pieces is their elegance: tailoring of the upholstered units is impeccable, and the shaping of the wood members has been done with an eye towards creating an impression of luxury. One of the finest of the chairs is the light armchair at the top of the page. Its frame is beautifully proportioned, and the combination of comfort and elegance, together with light weight, is excellent. Widdicomb Furniture Company, manufacturer.

Above: sofa in saffron-finished mahogany, produced in 1950.
Below: chair and ottoman, designed in 1948.

Dining group: The chairs have ladder backs, upholstered seats, completely exposed wood frames. T. H. Robsjohn-Gibbings, for The Widdicomb Furniture Company.

Dale Rooks

The photographs on these pages show furniture more recently designed by Robsjohn-Gibbings (1950 and 1951). While some of the feeling of the earlier designs is retained, and the use of rounded wood members is continued, the newer designs on the whole are less soft. There is also a slight suggestion of interest in furniture of the 17th century, notably in the reverse-taper legs of the tables above and in the heavy base of the table on the opposite page. The chairs also have deliberately been made less suave. T. H. Robsjohn-Gibbings, for Widdicomb Furniture Company.

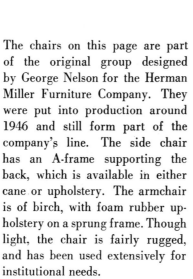

The chairs on this page are part of the original group designed by George Nelson for the Herman Miller Furniture Company. They were put into production around 1946 and still form part of the company's line. The side chair has an A-frame supporting the back, which is available in either cane or upholstery. The armchair is of birch, with foam rubber upholstery on a sprung frame. Though light, the chair is fairly rugged, and has been used extensively for institutional needs.

Chaise, chairs and a bench designed to suit the facilities of a wood-working plant in the Ozark region. The factory had originally made agricultural equipment, and one of its assets was the ability to bend relatively heavy wood members. As can be seen, the designer took advantage of this facility in virtually all of the pieces, which are made of solid oak and covered, for the most part, in woven oak withes. Designer: Edward D. Stone, for Fulbright Industries.

Armchair of bandsawed walnut with string back and seat. The chair is a highly personal expression of taste and has a distinctly individual kind of elegance. Irving Sabo, for the J. G. Furniture Company.

Herbert Matter

These chairs are part of the group of designs originally made by George Nakashima in his own workshop. Done in the manner of period chairs they have, nonetheless, a distinctly personal style which puts them out of the category of reproductions. They are built in birch, cherry or walnut and have mortised and tenoned joints. Knoll Associates.

An excellent lounge chair in birch, designed by Pierre Jeanneret, formerly the associate of Le Corbusier. The chair has detachable cushions which fasten in a most ingenious manner to the webbed support. Manufacturer: Knoll Associates.

Herbert Matter

One of the early Knoll chairs, noteworthy for its clean lines and excellent structural design. The standard model shown comes with an upholstered and sprung seat and an open back. It is also available in other combinations.

A very crisp and light desk chair, which is also made in a lounge version. For a duplicate of this chair in tubular metal by the same designer, see page 116. Franco Albini, designer; Knoll Associates, manufacturers.

The degree to which production methods and facilities can influence design is aptly demonstrated by the furniture on these two pages. The plant was one which had been in the manufacture of Colonial reproductions, and the designer made full use of its woodturning and shaping equipment. All of the examples shown are from the Predictor group, designed by Paul McCobb for the O'Hearn Manufacturing Company.

The extent to which the designer utilized his client's lathes (the main equipment of the plant) is clearly shown by the examples here. Relatively few parts fall outside the general category of turnings.

An interesting part of the project was the planning of the designs so that many parts could be made at one time and then cut to fit the required units. Despite the extreme limitations imposed by the available factory equipment, the designer succeeded in achieving a fresh and individual expression.

An officer's chair, shown in a New York apartment designed by Baldwin and Machado. The chair can be taken apart and packed in a bag, and it belongs to a type of utility seating found all over the world. A number of designers (see Hardoy chair, p. 24 and Knorr stool, p. 71) have been intrigued by the excellent qualities of this furniture. Here the usual seat and back of canvas have been replaced by hide. The tractor-seat stool in the background was designed by Baldwin-Machado. The chair was made by the Gold Medal Folding Furniture Company.

These demountable, adjustable lounge chairs were shown at the Triennale exposition of 1951 in Milan. Note the use of the exhibition background to demonstrate their various features. This type also has a long, international and anonymous design history and has considerable interest in connection with the contemporary interior.

A very rugged version of the officer's chair which uses the prototype for its styling interest rather than its light weight and demountability. Covers and arm rests are in leather. Designer: Edward Wormley, for the Dunbar Furniture Corporation of Indiana.

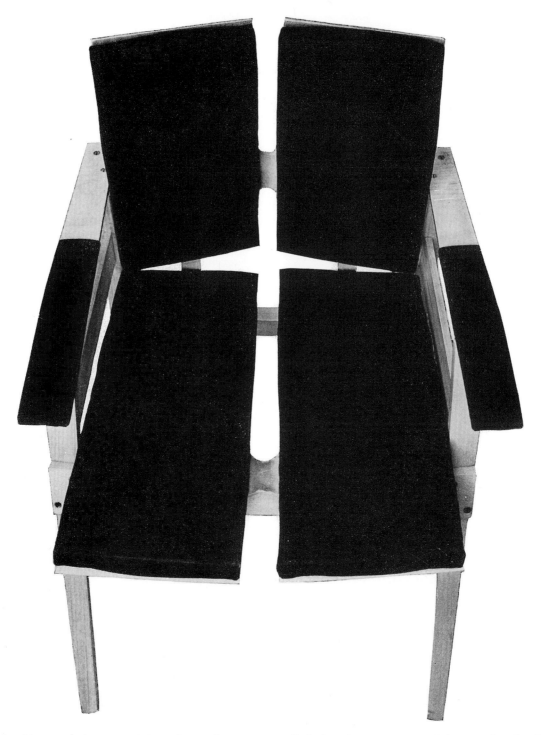

The ideas in this armchair are as interesting as its unusual appearance. The basic scheme was to provide extra seating comfort without springs, through the use of seat and back supports of very thin plywood padded with foam rubber. The plywood gives where weight is applied, but is strong enough not to break. By splitting both seat and back into two sections which are fastened to the frame by leather straps, further resilience is gained. Designers: Franco Albini, Luigi Colombini and Ezio Sgrelli, Italy.

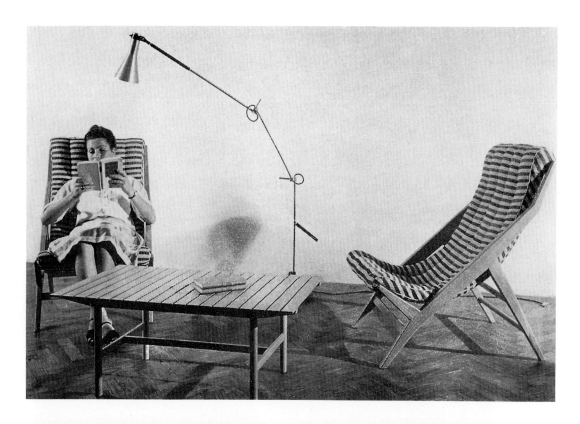

The side and lounge chairs shown above are also of recent Italian design. In both types the upholstery consists of pads covered in linen: wrapped around frames on the side chairs, suspended from frames on the reclining chairs. The decorative emphasis on the structure, common to both designs, is typical of a great deal of Italian work. Designer: Lucia Ponti Bonicalzi.

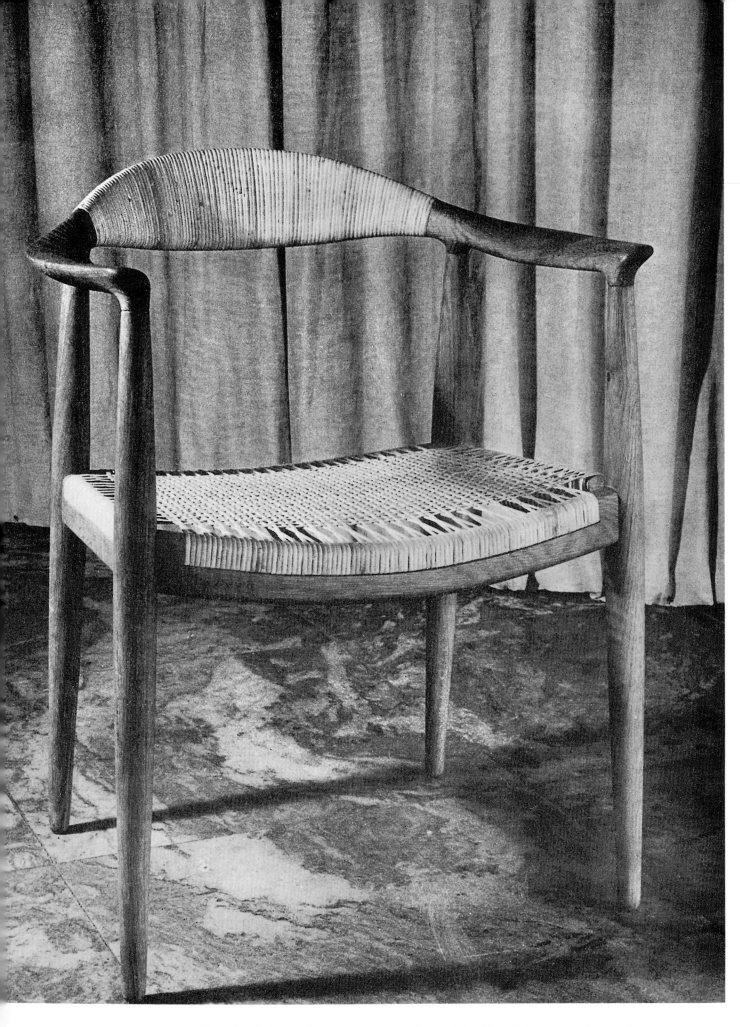

All of the chairs on these two pages are designed by Hans J. Wegner of Denmark, and made by Johannes Hansen. They represent a peak in the handicraft approach combined with a contemporary sense of form. The desk chair above is the most successful of the models shown in the U.S. Georg Jensen, importer.

Left, a lounge chair in hand-hewn smoked oak with a woven back and seat. Note the handles on the seat which may not be entirely useful, but certainly demonstrate the cabinetmaker's virtuosity. It would be interesting to compare this chair with the Barcelona chair (page 133) of Mies van der Rohe.

Below, a vigorous re-styling of the traditional Danish fan-backed chair. While the construction is fundamentally the same as in the original type, the proportions have been freely modified.

An excellent small armchair, simple in construction and relatively inexpensive. It represents one kind of thing a good designer is likely to come up with when the requirements are as listed above. Ray Komai, for the J. G. Furniture Company.

An armchair of the so-called "sculptured" type, an approach used by a number of designers to relieve what they consider undesirable severity. Designer: Milo Baughman, for Fine Arts Furniture Company.

Ben Schnall

A first-rate light desk chair. The frame is an excellent structure, well conceived for production and agreeably styled. Jens Risom, designer and manufacturer.

This wood armchair has not only been gracefully shaped but very carefully worked out to provide easily detached upholstery. Jens Risom, designer and manufacturer.

This handsome, low-backed desk chair was designed by Prof. R. Riemerschmid in 1899 and discovered and modified by Edward J. Wormley for the Dunbar Furniture Corporation of Indiana.

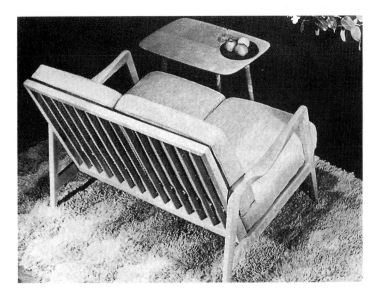

Knock-down chairs and sofas with loose cushions and removable slip covers. Keyhole type connectors are used for assembly. Folke Ohlsson, designer for Madress-Fabriken Dux. Swedish Modern, importer.

A number of seating pieces by the designer-manufacturer Jens Risom. They are of interest as designs made with an eye for institutional use, which requires furniture which is rugged, not too bulky and relatively neutral in appearance. The chair below, for instance, has straight-sided arms which allow its use as a sectional piece. The bench at the top combines real comfort with small size and sturdy construction.

Above, a birch chair with bent plywood back. The cushions tie to back and seat with criss-cross lacing. Metal rod braces are used for the legs. Chair (right) is of the sculptured variety already mentioned and is stiffened with x-type stretchers. Furniture of this kind requires extremely good craftsmanship for its successful realization. Designer: Harold M. Schwartz, for Romweber.

A subtly-shaped chair which combines a teak frame with a gray canvas cover and vermilion cushion. The high back is more commonly found in European than in U. S. furniture. Ib Kofod-Larsen, designer; Jacob Kjaer, cabinetmaker, Denmark.

All Scandinavian furniture tends to have the common look one might expect in a part of the world where cultural traditions are closely shared by several countries, but it is possible to find regional or national differences within the whole. The Danish character, for instance, shows up at the present time in a liking for highly articulated designs and in the refined detailing of each part. Two of its leading exponents are Finn Juhl and Hans Wegner, both now well known in the U.S., both designers who delight in woodworking at the virtuoso level. Their influence on furniture design here has already been considerable and may still increase. This development will not prove an unmixed blessing, for work of this type requires a degree of skill, patience and integrity not too common in the U.S. furniture industry. For the successful realization of the kind of thing shown here the collaboration of the best cabinetmakers is a necessity.

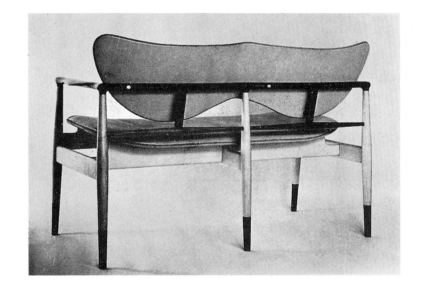

A settee designed some years ago by Finn Juhl. Note the separation of seat, back and frame, also the beautiful detailing of individual parts. Niels Vodder, cabinetmaker.

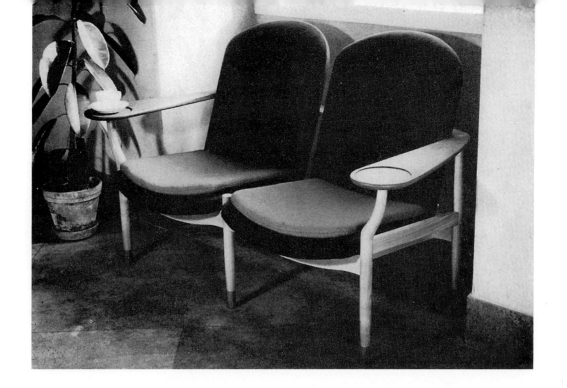

The arm rests on this settee are useful for cups, glasses and ashtrays. Here the articulation has been carried to the point of separating the seats. Note the tipped legs, almost standard in Danish work. Borge Mogensen, designer; Erhard Rasmussen, cabinetmaker.

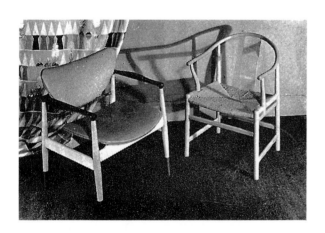

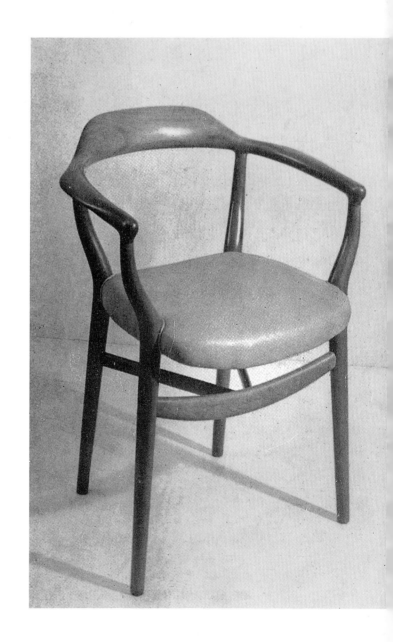

Above, an early chair by Finn Juhl (left) and a modernized traditional chair by Hans Wegner. Right, another early design by Finn Juhl. It is interesting to compare this with Juhl's later work.

It was remarked before that the Danish influence on U.S. furniture was not without its drawbacks and dangers. In the work shown on these four pages we have the exception—furniture designed by Finn Juhl and produced by Baker Furniture Incorporated. The designs are among the best Juhl has turned out and it is hard to see how the execution could leave anything further to be desired.

In this collection, which is fairly sizable, the characteristics noted earlier appear in a highly developed form. Boldly carved shapes are in evidence in almost all of the pieces. The articulation of separate parts could hardly be carried much farther than in the sofa in the photograph above, where the separate backrest becomes a major design element. For grace and elegance neither Juhl nor his colleagues in Denmark have produced a better chair than the piece at the right.

The chair at the right was done about three years before the piece on the facing page. While similar in concept, it lacks the crisp smoothness of the later design. Furniture in the Baker line is in English sycamore (an almost white wood) and walnut, and the two woods are often combined in the same piece. Finishes are as close to natural as the requirements of practical use will allow.

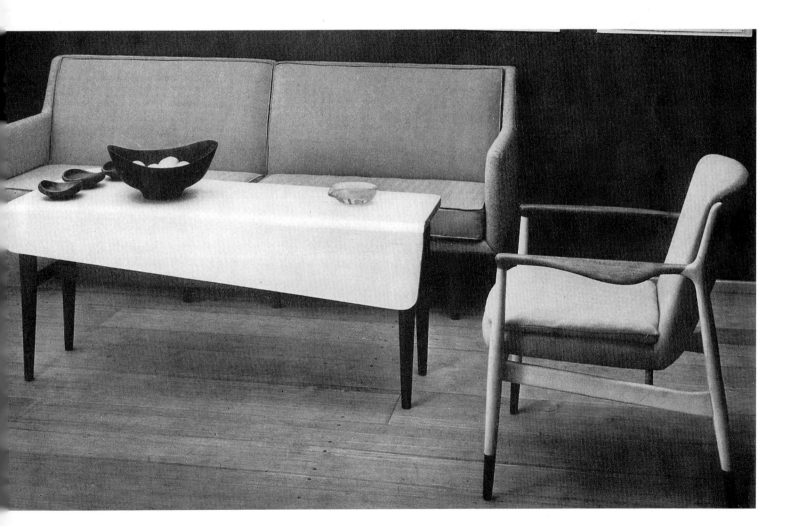

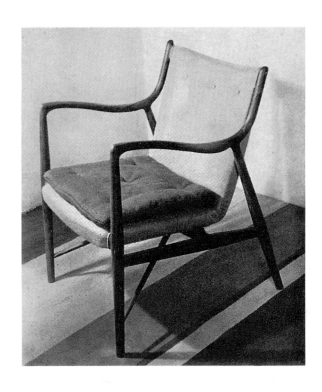

Although the cabinet work in his furniture is its most immediately recognizable feature, the designer says "I was never trained to design anything but houses, which seems to have influenced me, so that I look at any piece of furniture as a construction based on the natural character of the material, more than as a collection of cabinetmaker's joints, as many furniture designers are apt to do." The point is well made, for the structural character of the furniture is quite evident. It is equally evident, however, that the designer's preoccupations go well beyond construction. If one compared this chair with one of the Eames chairs (also designed with an eye to the structure) there is a significant difference in the initial approach as well as in the final cost. The approach in this furniture is essentially that of the handicraftsman and it shares the advantages and disadvantages of the handicraft method.

The settings for the furniture in Baker Furniture's Grand Rapids showroom were also designed by Finn Juhl.

metal

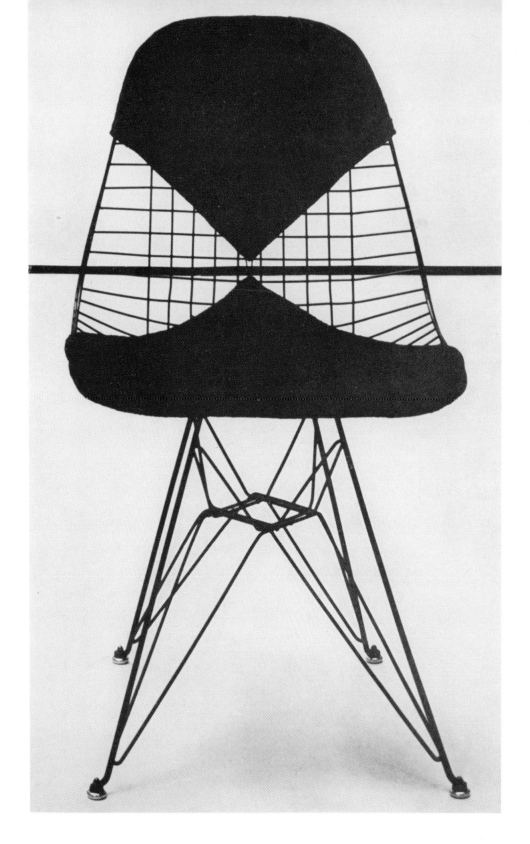

The wire shell is the third major accomplishment of Charles Eames in his continuing effort to develop high quality mass production furniture at low cost. This piece, which comes only in the side chair form shown here, is made in much the same way as wire displays, baskets, etc., being laid up and welded, and then formed. Two forms of snap-on upholstery have been designed, the economy version shown in silhouette above, and the other (right) which covers the whole shell. Bases are for the most part the same as the ones offered with the plastic shell (see page 56), and the materials used include wire, wire and wood, and steel rod. Upholstery is either leather or fabric. Herman Miller Furniture Company.

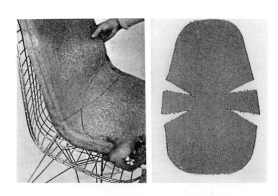

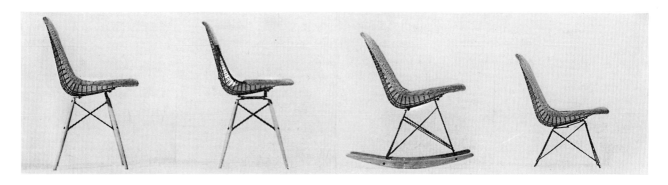

The various bases create (left to right) a side chair, swivel chair, rocker and lounge chair.

A dining chair of welded metal rod combined with solid wood. This rather difficult mixture of dissimilar materials has been handled most successfully. Designer: Paul McCobb, for Winchendon Furniture Company.

One of a small group of outdoor pieces. The structure consists of one rod forming the back, arms and front legs; this is supported by welded-on back legs. The seat is held up by wires. Designer: George Nelson for Arbuck.

Wicker-woven backs on wrought iron frames are used on these side chairs, part of a group designed by Tempestini for the John B. Salterini Company.

Attractive and comfortable dining chairs in wrought iron, with steel mesh used on the backs as an exposed decorative element. The chairs are made in both black and white finishes. Designer: Harry Lawenda for Kneedler-Fauchère.

The furniture shown here was the subject of a project given students in industrial design at the Chouinard Art Institute in Los Angeles. Enameled steel frames are fitted with canvas seats and backs. Designers: Bernard Flagg and Kipp Stewart. Manufacturer (chair only): J. G. Furniture Company.

The pieces shown on these two pages represent one of the most distinguished groups of metal furniture in production. The project began very modestly as a small venture on the West coast and the collection has gradually expanded, now including some very fresh and attractive designs. Basically the group consists of tubular metal structures, finished in cord, expanded metal, upholstery, woven rattan and redwood. In a few instances steel rods or bars replace the tubing. Seating types include side chairs, armchairs, lounge units (with or without footstools) and the large reclining platform shown above. The metal frames are produced in black, "lobster" red and a "grapefruit" yellow. Designers: Hendrik Van Keppel and Taylor Green; manufacturer: Van Keppel-Green.

This patented chair has a number of unusual features. The tubular steel frame, which has been given a rather uncommon shape, serves as a kind of scaffold on which a canvas bag is hung. Both seat and back of this bag have plywood inserts for stiffness. When the canvas is in place, it in turn supports two loose cushions whose covers can be removed for cleaning. Designer: Marco Zanuso, Italy.

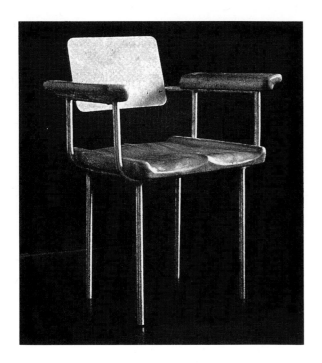

In this chair an attempt has been made to combine the shapes of structural steel tubing and heavily carved solid wood. The result is more interesting for the idea than its appearance. Designer: E. Sottsass Jr., Italy.

A stacking chair of French origin, made of chrome-plated steel and interlaced cord. It is by far the most beautiful of the recent chairs in this material. Designer: Andre Dupré, for Knoll Associates.

Herbert Matter

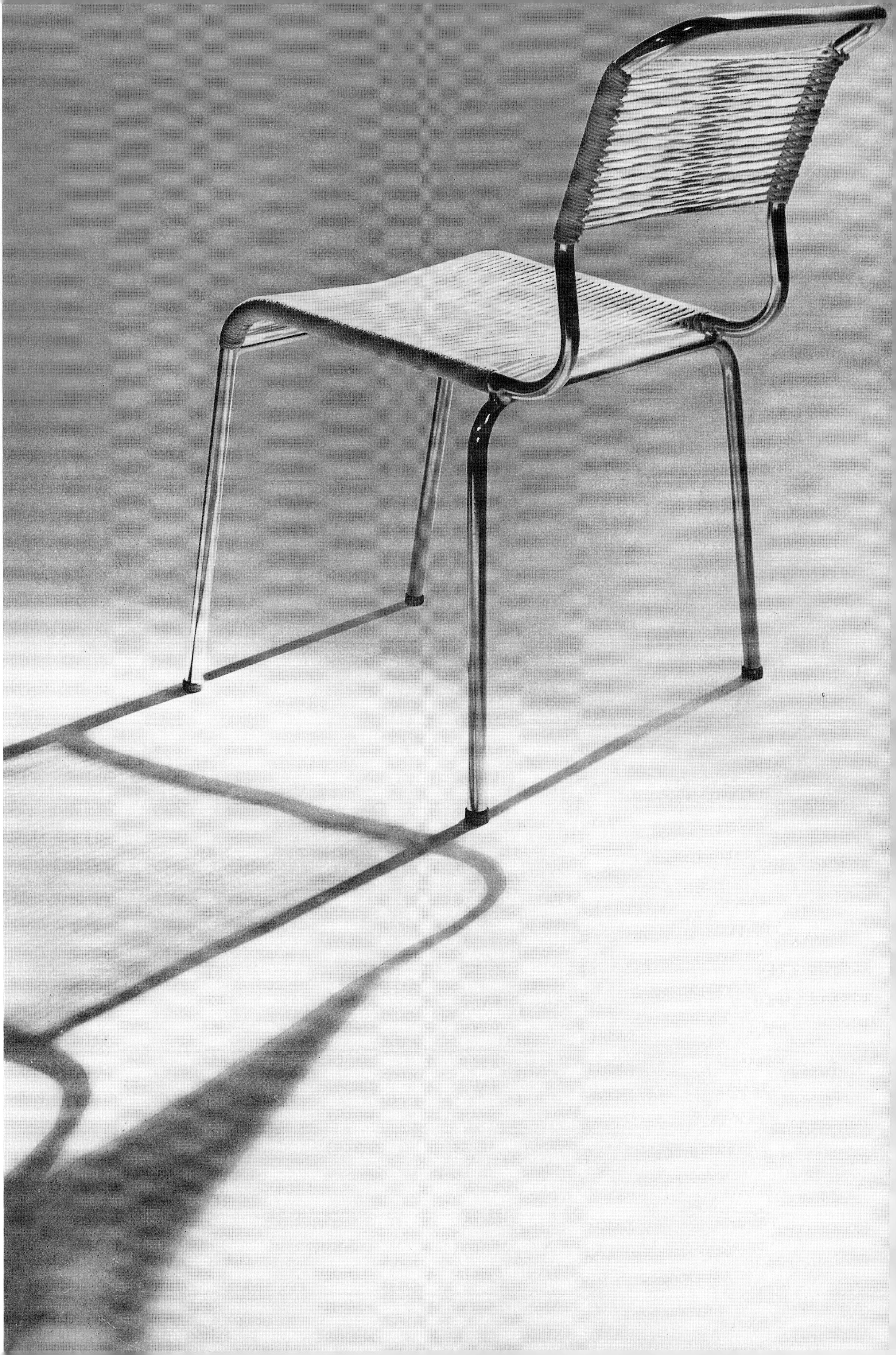

Midori

These three chairs represent an attempt to use ordinary steel angles for seating units. Oddly enough, this common material, which must of necessity be put together in straight pieces, results in pieces of considerable formality, an impression accentuated by the combination with wood and cane. The two chairs above are both suitable for desk use or dining; the upholstered chair at the right has been set at lounge chair height. Designer: George Nelson, for Herman Miller Furniture Company.

The dining chair below deviates in some respects from standard practice in metal furniture design. Its frame for instance, is made of aluminum rod rather than tubular steel, a change which contributes to the relatively light weight of the piece. It also has fully sprung and upholstered seat and back, thus providing a kind of comfort normally found in heavier pieces. Designer: George Nelson, for Herman Miller Furniture Company.

4671 *19" w. 20½" d. 31½" h.*

Dale Rooks

Maurice Martiné, designer and manufacturer.

In many metal chairs, as in the earlier designs in wood, one frequently comes across designs which maintain a sharp distinction between the supporting frame or cradle and the seating unit proper. Three different examples of this approach are shown on this page. At the top left is a fully upholstered seat and back set into a metal frame of the springy type. At the left is a lighter frame of wood and white cord combined with a rigid carrier of steel. The chair directly below is a seat and back unit, upholstered in the conventional manner, supported by a black metal cradle which also provides an arm rest.

Ben Schnall

Jens Risom, designer and manufacturer.

A two-seater, upholstered like two separate units, with a framework of brass or copper. Alfred Blake, designer.

Removable canvas covers for seat and back make this outdoor chair particularly practical. Designer: Milo Baughman. Both chairs shown here are manufactured by Pacific Iron Products.

Two of the prize-winning chairs submitted in the low cost furniture competition sponsored by the Museum of Modern Art. The chair above is an interesting experiment in the use of inflated tubes within a cloth envelope as a way of getting seating comfort inexpensively. The frame folds and the chair presumably could be shipped deflated as well as knocked down. Davis J. Platt, designer. Left, a scoop chair made of a sheet of metal bent around and seamed in the back. It is sold with and without its upholstered pad. Don J. Knorr, designer. Manufacturer: Knoll Associates.

One of the very best of the metal armchairs, by one of the very best of the contemporary Italian designers. The chair is characterized by great precision of detail and delicacy of form. The junction between the arm and front leg, for instance, ordinarily handled as a bend in tubular steel is here a welded joint. This is more expensive, obviously, but the appearance could not have been achieved in any other way. Franco Albini, the designer, is also responsible for the interior. The chair, with very slight modifications, is manufactured here by Knoll Associates.

Black wrought iron used in combination with natural Italian wicker on wood frames. The furniture has more richness of texture than is customarily found in the so-called "garden" category. Designer: Maurizio Tempestini, for John B. Salterini.

Another example of separate frame and seating unit. Here a rather complex structure of tubular steel receives seat and back cushions in foam rubber. Designers: Mariani and Perogalli.

These wire shell chairs are by the designer—Harry Bertoia—who is a sculptor, and a distinguished one. Yet the strong sculptural quality of these pieces stems less from Mr. Bertoia's special interests than from a general situation already noted earlier in this book: the lack of usable walls in the contemporary interior. Glass exteriors and open plans have combined to force seating furniture out into the open, and have thus created a need for pieces modeled in the round. Chairs designed in this manner, lacking the conventional, sharply defined front, sides and back, inevitably take on the character of sculpture.

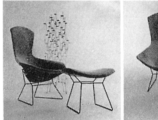

The structure of the Bertoia chairs is wire and rod. The former is welded into an open mesh and shaped. Upholstery is molded foam rubber covered on all sides with fabric. The final chair is hence a combination of two shells, one structural, one supported.

An interesting special feature is a rubber connector between shell and frame which permits the chair to swing in its cradle from an upright to a reclining position. The use of rubber as a kind of spring connector has already been seen in commercial desk chairs, but this appears to be the first successful application to domestic furniture.

The group contains four pieces—a side chair, a low armchair, a high-backed chair and an ottoman. Metal shells and cradles are sold in two finishes—black or white—and upholstery is provided in the forms shown in the illustrations. Manufacturer: Knoll Associates.

Herbert Matter

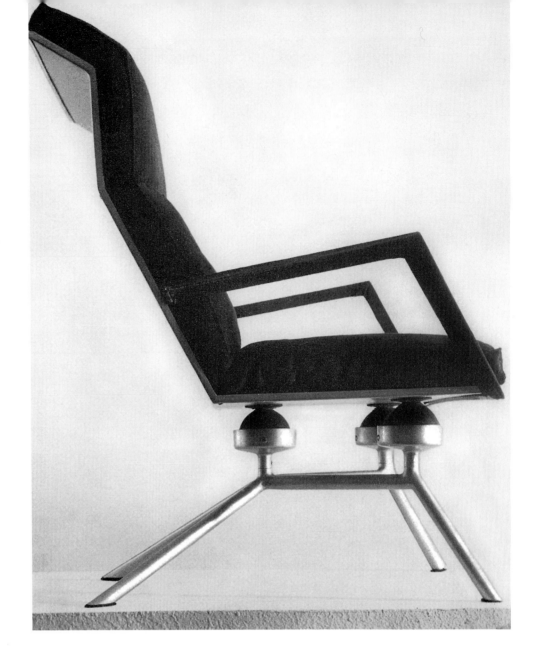

This chair is a good example of the way ideas emerge simultaneously. Developed in Italy during the war, the design was complete when the interchange of publications between the U.S. and Italy was resumed, and photographs of it were among the first to arrive here. It was in the same period that the Eames chair was designed and completed, and there was no possibility whatever that either designer could have been aware of the other's work. Yet the rubber shock mount, even to the three-point suspension, figures prominently in each design. The resemblance between the chairs ceases here, of course, but the similarity in thinking is a striking coincidence.

Two uses of the Italian shock mount are shown here. Above, an all-metal armchair, with the crisp contours favored by many of the designers, is poised over a tubular steel base capped by three of the rubber connectors. On the facing page is an office chair with a solid wood seat and plywood back, supported by a single rubber connector. The side chair uses sheet metal, slung like canvas between front and back supporting members. Designers: Cristiani and Fratino.

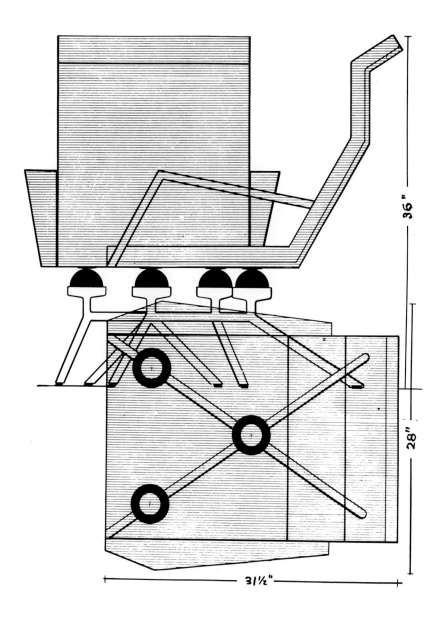

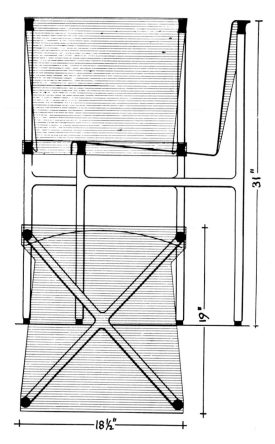

121

The tripod stool shown below is a modernized version of the folding wood - and - canvas stool used by painters and others for decades. The chairs appear to be more experimental in a sculptural than in a technical sense. Designer: Dennis Lennon, England.

Nigel Henderson

Hans Van Nes

These nesting chairs of welded magnesium are probably the lightest in production anywhere—a half-dozen of them can easily be lifted with one hand. They are also exceedingly strong. They were originally designed for use in naval hospital ships, where the qualities mentioned are required along with ease of cleaning. The chair has a seat and back of canvas, and both are simply removed; the back lifts off the rod frame and the seat is a flap which is laced underneath. Because of the special advantages of this chair, it has gradually been brought into wider use. Above, it is seen in the New York store of Bonwit Teller. Designer: Jack Heany; manufacturer: Treitel-Gratz; distributor: Herman Miller.

123

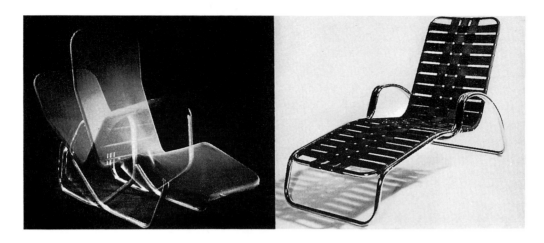

The famous "Barwa" reclining chair is shown in its two positions by a multiple-exposure photograph. Construction is canvas over tubular aluminum frame. Designers: Edgar Bartolucci and Jack Waldheim for Barwa Sales.

A webbed chaise, widely used as an outdoor or porch chair. It is interesting to compare this commercial product with the earlier, more experimental types. Designer: Alice Roth, for The Troy Sunshade Company.

  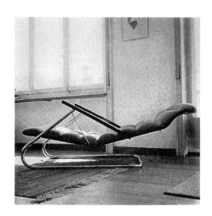

This adjustable chair was designed by a young Swiss architect for his own use. As illustrated in the three photographs above, it assumes the positions of a lounge chair, reclining chair and a contoured platform. The construction appears to be very simple, with the adjustments being made by means of a sliding connection to the chair arm. The upholstery is removable. Designer: Otto Kolb.

An extreme development within the current vogue for black iron, this chair has been made entirely of the one material. A sling of woven steel mesh is welded to the rod frame. Designer: Sol Bloom, for New Dimensions Furniture, Inc.

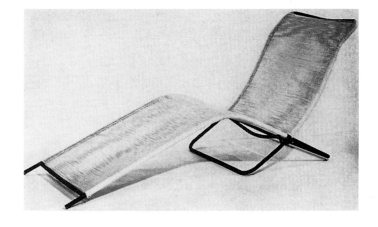

Below: "Hairpin" type of side chair, in which the design of the frame gives great resilience to the back and incidentally demonstrates the considerable strength of steel rod construction. Designer: Dorothy Schindele, for Modern Color, Inc.

An outdoor folding chair with a tubular steel frame strung with cord. The unit is made available in a variety of colors. Designer: Greta Magnusson Grossman, for Modern Color, Inc.

A variation on the Bauhaus type of tubular chair. George Nelson, for Herman Miller Furniture Company.

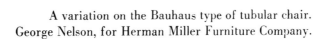

A folding chair for either indoor or outdoor use. The steel frame is finished in black, red, gray or green. Designer: Russel Wright, for Schwayder Bros.

A folding chair which has the unusual added feature of a self-adjusting seat and back. Designers: Albini, Colombini and Sgrelli, Italy.

Winning design in the 1952 competition for furniture sponsored by the National Gallery of Canada in association with the Aluminum Company of Canada and the Canadian Lumbermen's Association. A most intelligently conceived chair, which uses wood, plywood and aluminum tubing in a workable and attractive combination. Designer: Lawrie McIntosh.

A decorative approach to the upholstered metal-frame chair. The joint between the X and the seat frame is possible only in welded steel. Designer: Tony Paul, for Robert Barber.

Italian wicker on a wrought iron frame. Designer: Maurizio Tempestini, for John B. Salterini Company.

Cord woven into a net was used here to give maximum emphasis to the linear design of the chair frame. Designers: Painter-Teague-Petertil, for Pacific Iron Products.

A sturdy side chair, made of bar stock. The plastic seat and back are laced to the frame. Robert Brown for Brown-Jordan.

Herbert Matter

The most interesting thing about this Swedish work chair is the absence of any effort to hide or gloss over the details of its construction. The designer obviously was searching for an economical manufacturing solution, and the results of his search are clearly visible. The same general approach is to be found in the work of a number of Scandinavian and Italian designers. Odelberg-Olsen, designer; Knoll Associates, importer.

A comparison between this U.S. design and its Swedish counterpart is instructive. It shows, among other things, that the U.S. approach is to take the mechanics for granted, and hence this chair does about the same job as the other, but with much less emphasis on its working parts. However, it lacks the Swedish chair's consistent expression of style. Cramer Posture Chair Company.

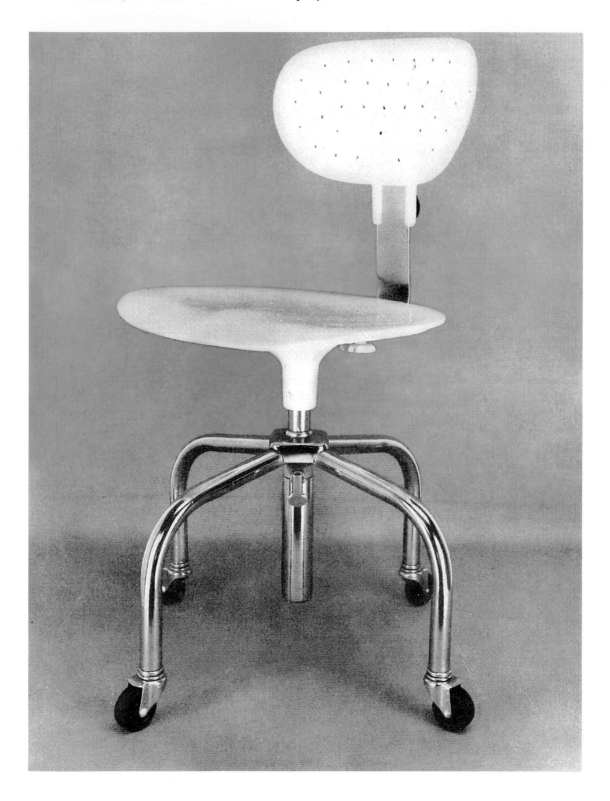

The manufacturer of this low-backed chair has specialized in furniture reminiscent of the Orient, and here, in spite of the fact that a modern material (rectangular steel tubing) has been employed for the structural frame, the oriental feeling persists. Designer: Harry Lawenda, for Kneedler-Fauchère.

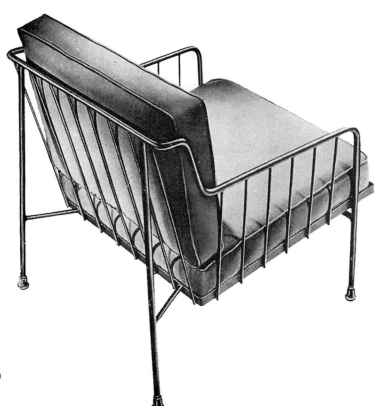

A lounge-chair companion piece to the armchair shown on page 106. In both the sling principle (seat suspended from a frame by welded steel rods) is used. Designer: George Nelson, for Arbuck, Inc.

The chair which has an attached shelf or table is a type which goes back to the 17th century and possibly even earlier, and the number of variations which have been tried out is legion. Its traditional advantages—apart from lecture-hall use—are that it takes over many of the functions of the end table. Here a combination of wood and metal has produced a rather primitive but agreeable effect. Designer: Dennis Lennon, England.

Le Corbusier—1928

Marcel Breuer—1925

Shown on these pages are several of the important chair designs of the 1925-30 period, a time when several countries, notably Germany, were making important new contributions. The chairs of Breuer and Le Corbusier show a certain similarity in the way stretched fabric has been used with tubular frames. Two of the chairs of Mies van der Rohe appear in the Tugendhat house interior, and the most famous of them all is again illustrated on the facing page.

Mies van der Rohe—1929-1930

Mies van der Rohe's "Barcelona" chair is named after the International Exposition held in that city in 1929, where his pavilion for the German government instantly gained world recognition as one of the great achievements of modern architecture. The chair, like all of his buildings and furniture, has been designed with the most painstaking attention to detail, and demands perfect execution. Its frame is of polished stainless steel; supporting straps are of saddle leather; the leather-covered cushions are self-welted. One of the most costly pieces in production, it has no substitute where the height of elegance is the aim of the interior designer. Manufacturer: Knoll Associates.

Above and below, Sol-Air furniture for both indoor and outdoor use, designed by Swanson Associates (Pipsan Saarinen Swanson and Robert Swanson) for Ficks-Reed.

Above, a chair made of welded square tubing, lacquered in charcoal, off-white, gunmetal, olive, and gray. The base is webbed to support the foam rubber cushions. Designer: William Armbruster, for Edgewood Furniture Company.

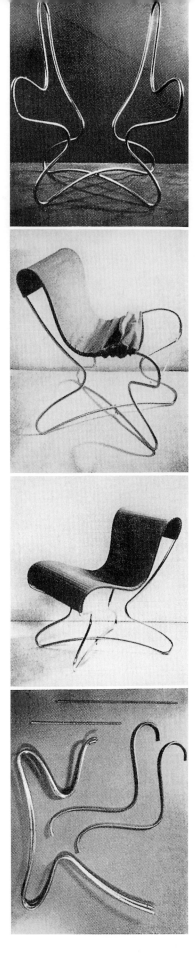

A student project, developed at the Institute of Design in Chicago. Note the use of one length of bent stainless steel to form two legs and a back support. The resilient back characteristic of so many metal-frame chairs is also seen here.

Below, a steel and saddle leather chair as shown at the 1951 Good Design exhibit in Chicago. The steel supporting members make a frame over which seat and back are stretched. Ron Fidler Associates, designers and manufacturers.

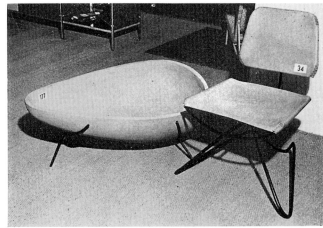

Fran Byrne

Four views of an unusual steel chair. It is claimed that the even distribution of stresses allows the use of especially thin (9/16″) tubing. The cover is plastic, with zip-on fastenings. The entire unit is demountable. Designer: Eva Zeisel; Richards Morgenthau, distributor.

This two-seater is a companion piece to the "Antelope" nesting chairs used in the 1951 Exposition in London. The delicacy of the design recalls the old ice cream parlor chairs in wire. Designer: Ernest Race; Waldron Associates, distributors.

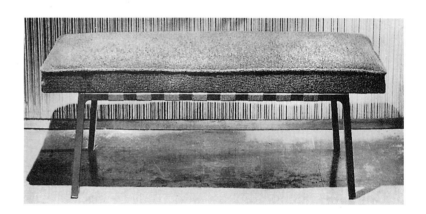

The webbed steel base above, used as shown here for an upholstered bench, has been standardized for coffee table use as well. Designer: William Armbruster, for Edgewood Furniture Company.

A combination piece, in which the same frame supports seat, back and shelf. The idea of a long table for lamps, magazines, etc., behind a couch is one which used to be popular and still has advantages. Designer: Paolo A. Chessa, Italy.

These three-legged stools in birch and white enameled steel have been designed for stacking. Designer: Florence Knoll, for Knoll Associates.

Another type of stacking stool, in black iron and laced saddle leather. Designers: Robert Englebrecht and John A. Holabird, Jr., for Interior Trend Associates.

The treatment of bracing members into major elements of design gives this settee its special character. The same vocabulary has been used for chairs and tables. Designer: Darrell Landrum for Avard.

This stacking chair was extensively used at the 1951 Festival of Britain. It is an economical and sturdy piece, with curved plywood seat and back on a welded tubular steel frame. The seat is lightly padded and covered with plastic. The chair looks better in groups (illustration below) than as a single piece. Designer: Robin Day; distributor: J. G. Furniture Company.

The all-metal chair above was designed for the Swiss National Exposition of 1939 and is still one of the best of its kind. Seat and back are formed from a single sheet of perforated aluminum. Hans Coray, designer. P. & W. Blattmann, manufacturer.

Three kinds of open-work chairs used at the 1951 Festival of Britain. Ernest Race, designer. Waldron Associates, distributors.

Design Research Unit

Herbert Matter

The so-called "Hardoy" chair is one of the most famous of modern designs, and it is unique in its combination of sculptural quality and comfort. The entire chair is nothing more than a continuous metal frame on which a kind of pouch of fabric or leather is slung. One of the most inexpensive chairs to fabricate, it is now being made by a number of companies. The original version shown here, adapted from an Italian officer's chair which had a leather seat and wood frame, was manufactured by Knoll Associates. Designers: Hardoy, Bonet and Kurchan.

Two stacking chairs in tubular steel are shown at the left and below. Designer: Alice Roth, for the Troy Sunshade Company.

A custom chair, designed for use in a small dining room. Half-round strips of wood on canvas (a construction similar to that of the old roll-top desk cover) are suspended from a tubular frame. Designers: Architects Associated.

Originally designed by the architects for the Birmingham, Michigan, High School, this stacking chair is now being produced for general institutional use. Swanson Associates, designers; American Seating Company, manufacturer.

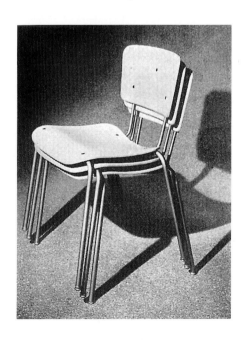

Little has been heard from Japan in the area of chair design for the very good reason that the Japanese, traditionally, do not use chairs. However, in their renewed enthusiasm for things Western, Japan's architects appear to be turning more and more to Occidental types of modern houses, and to the chair, not so much as a seating device as a symbol.

The bamboo-and-steel chair at the top shows an interesting adaptation of traditional weaving of bamboo, in a new application. It was designed for export by sculptor Isamu Noguchi. Another interpretation, a mesh cradle on a metal frame, is by the Japanese painter and designer, Guen Iyokuma.

Above, an early model of a sling chair with a built-in cushion of foam rubber. At the right is shown the version which was produced in the U.S. As a design the chair relates to the Hardoy (in spite of the different kind of seating it offers) and the early slung canvas chairs of Breuer and Le Corbusier (see page 132). The three-legged chair in metal and hinged plywood is by the same designer, and despite its interesting appearance, shares the disadvantages of other three-legged chairs. Designer: Paolo A. Chessa, for J. G. Furniture Company.

upholstery

Three separate units make up the chair illustrated above, an upholstered seat, a wood frame and an attached sliding tray. The piece was developed for use in a nursery in Britain. R. D. Russell and R. Y. Goodden, designers.

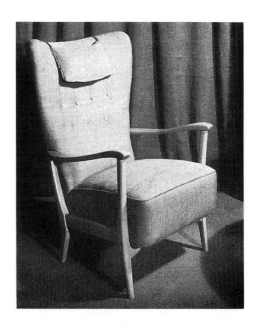

The wing chair at the right, with its soft contours and its attached pillow is typical in every way of a kind of chair which has been manufactured for years in Scandinavia. The knock-down construction, difficult to achieve in a chair of this shape and size, is important where export is a factor. Importer: Swedish Modern.

Furniture, this page, from Knoll Associates.

Upholstered furniture, notoriously more difficult to handle in an interesting way than the lighter seating units, has shown a definite tendency to parallel some of the important design developments in chairs. Most conspicuous, perhaps, is the articulation of seat and frame. In some instances, as in the examples on the facing page, this separation is functional, reflecting the need for knock-down construction. In others it may stem from a desire to simplify production of the different components, or from a wish to achieve a design whose appearance is lighter. The furniture at the top of this page is a good example of the scale and proportion of the newer types of upholstered seating.

A daybed, with a foam rubber mattress on a wood platform. There is a foot pedal which operates the back rest, opening the unit to full sleeping width. Designer: Richard Stein, for Knoll Associates.

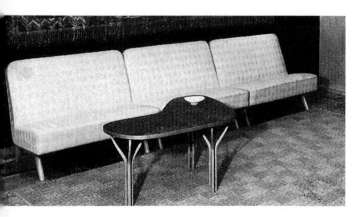

Both illustrations show furniture designed for the public spaces of the Hotell Malmen in Stockholm. Not only do they represent an unusually high design standard for work in this category, but the chairs above have an interest which goes beyond this limited application. Constructed as fully upholstered shells, they can be removed easily from their cradles to simplify cleaning, refinishing or repair. What the wood frames appear to lack in elegance they make up in rigidity. Carl-Axel Acking, designer.

It is unusual to find folding chairs with this degree of comfort, and it may be assumed that the folding feature is of greater value in shipping than in daily use. Note how the legs have been angled to fit together when stacked. Lined up as shown, the chairs can form settees of indefinite length. Ole Wanscher, designer; John Stuart, distributor.

The curved X-frame of this armchair supports an unusually comfortable seating shell. Here, too, the pivoted members of oak offer the advantages of folding construction. Franco Albini, designer.

The only difference between the articulated cradles of wood and of metal lies in the much lighter appearance of the latter. The examples above, designed by Chon Gregory for The Arrow Upholstery Company, are upholstered units of conventional construction set on cradles of bent and welded steel.

The frame of the chair at the right—also steel—is furnished in chrome, brass or black finish. Designer: Harold Bartos, for Lehigh Furniture Company.

Chair in foam rubber on an iron frame.
Designer: Joe Martin, for Robert Barber.

Designer: Robert McKean, for Gallo Original Iron Works, Inc.

The conversion of traditional wrought iron garden furniture into all - purpose household furniture has taken place with remarkable speed, and it may be attributed at least in part to the broad shift in taste towards modern design and materials. The chair at the left uses an all-metal frame, with the skeleton very much in evidence. The same frame, covered in woven rattan, expanded metal or redwood slats, serves for both indoor and outdoor use. Designers: Hendrik Van Keppel and Taylor Green, for Van Keppel-Green.

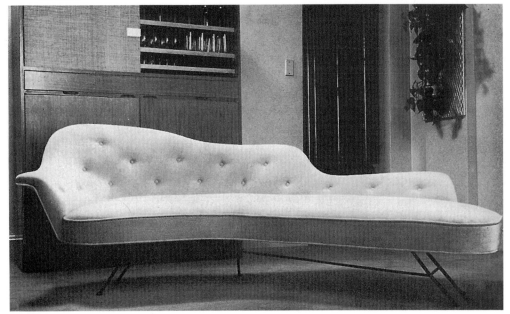

A custom chaise with an almost period look despite the metal cradle. The piece was designed for a small living room which required light-looking but generous seating. Designers: Architects Associated.

The huge sofa, and its accompanying ottoman, look as much like sculpture as seating but the designs lend themselves easily to standard upholstering methods. Both the size and design of the pieces restrict their use to large interiors. Designer: Isamu Noguchi, for the Herman Miller Furniture Company.

The emergence of molding techniques in furniture (particularly in light chairs) has had an effect on the design of the heavier upholstered seating as well. All of the examples on these pages and some of the following show an effort to develop shapes which look as if the customary wood frame had been eliminated. Since in most instances the frame is still there, the designs may perhaps be considered anticipations of future molded production. The chair and ottoman are by S. H. Vakassian and Sons.

Armchair and love seat of conventional design,
using molded foam rubber on springs. Pascoe.

A wing chair without arms, designed by Elias
Svedberg for Knoll Associates. The knockdown
table is also by the same designer.

The background is a mock-up of a ship's interior, created to enable the designer to check on the suitability of the furniture. A variety of pieces is shown here, including a sofa with a separate back rest. Designer: Dirk van Sliedregt, for the H. H. de Klerk Furniture Company of Holland.

The sofa in the back is one of a number of upholstered pieces, modifications of existing models, by Carter Winter for the J. G. Furniture Company. The light armchair was designed by Ray Komai for the same manufacturer.

One of the very few "sculptured" pieces of upholstered furniture whose form relates directly to an inner shell of molded plastic. A skin of foam rubber is laid over the shell and is covered, in turn, by fabric. Designer: Eero Saarinen, for Knoll Associates.

An excellent example of the "anticipatory" type of design referred to earlier. Here the "shell look" has been achieved, but through use of a complex wood frame. In appearance the piece is modern but in construction (like most furniture in this category) it is entirely traditional. Designer: Finn Juhl.

The deep upholstered pieces grouped here show very clearly what has happened to the so-called "overstuffed" chair and sofa. Bulk has been taken out, lines have been straightened and shapes have been simplified. High legs are most effective in reducing apparent weight. In the settee at the right, designed by Florence Knoll, loose cushions are set on a sprung base; in the other examples cushions and spring platform are combined in a single unit. All the furniture on this page is from Knoll Associates.

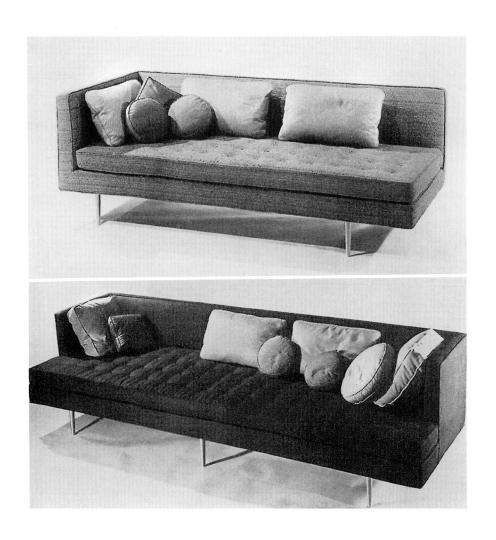

Three pieces by one of the leading U.S. designers, Edward Wormley, all representative of his highly developed personal style. The sofa at the top, fitted with only one arm, suggests many possible combinations with tables, storage units and other furniture. The piece in the center is nine feet long and would be a most luxurious element in an interior scaled for it: The daybed shown at the bottom has a reversible mattress. Manufacturer: Dunbar Furniture Corporation of Indiana.

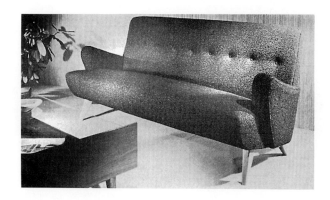

The sofa and armchair, like other pieces shown in this section, represent a re-styling of traditional types. The tailored look which characterizes them, as well as the effort to reduce bulk and weight, fits the requirements of the contemporary interior. Jens Risom, designer and manufacturer.

Ben Schnall

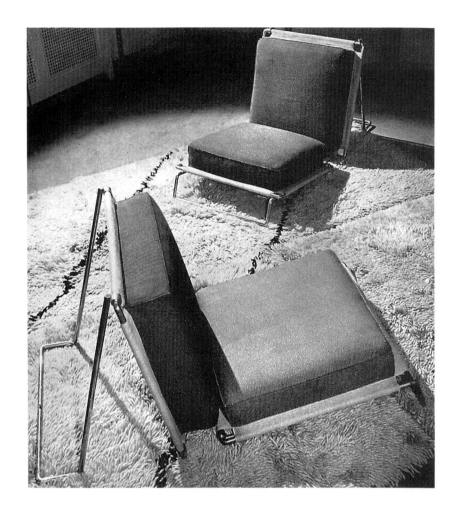

Two-piece chairs with brass frames and canvas covers. Cushions are loose. Designers: Ernesto Rogers and Ignazio Gardella, Italy.

If one extends the present trend towards more informality, reflected in the appearance of more and more furniture for lounging rather than for sitting, then the kind of thing shown on these pages represents one set of logical conclusions. The chairs lose their legs, acquire adjustable, hospital bed-type frames (right) or simply become cushions on the floor. Furniture of this kind requires clothing suitable for it. It is curious that as the Japanese turn to chairs after centuries of sitting on the floor, we should start moving in exactly the opposite direction.

Foam rubber mattress on adjustable frame. Designed by the firm of Banfi, Belgioiso, Peresutti and Rogers, Italy.

Three hinged cushions, which can be propped up as shown to make a seat with its own backrest. They can also be folded over to form an ottoman or spread out flat. Designer: Edward J. Wormley, for Dunbar Furniture Corporation of Indiana.

The idea here is similar to the one above. The piece was designed to serve as a low daybed for a girl's room, but can be used as an ottoman, backrest, floor mattress and so on. Designers: Neville Ward and Frank Austin, England.

One of the first of the modern daybeds, this platform type of seating has since become an integral part of the modern design vocabulary. The original of this model was built in 1941 by the designer for his own use, and it served its purpose very well for eight years before the idea of putting it into production suggested itself. The daybed now in production does not have the webbed base shown in the photograph: the webbing base has been replaced by a spring platform which has greater resilience and none of the webbing's tendency to sag. Both mattress and bolsters are made of foam rubber. At left, an armchair and ottoman of conventional construction. Facing page, a number of upholstered pieces in the same group. The furniture at the top right is of interest as a combination of seating with attached tables and other accessories. Designer: George Nelson, for the Herman Miller Furniture Company.

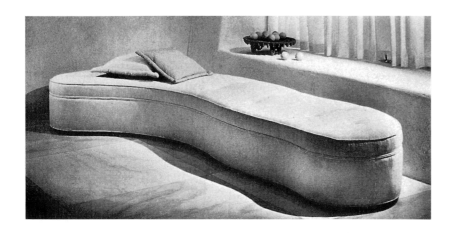

A number of pieces designed by Robsjohn-Gibbings. The sofa and the chaise were done a few years ago and reflect the designer's preference for crisp shapes and a tailored appearance. The piece at the top—it is difficult to find a name for it, as it does not fall into the usual categories—is a long, narrow upholstered platform with an irregular contour whose function would not be unlike that of the large Noguchi sofa on page 153. Such furniture as this, while hardly usable in the average domestic interior, nevertheless has a place in the contemporary scene. Manufacturer: Widdicomb Furniture Company.

All of the furniture shown here belongs to a variant of the sectional type. The intention is to achieve a "Built-in" look and, at the same time, an effect of size and luxury through the incorporation of curved sections. The units, which are concave, convex and straight along their front edges, can be combined to make a great variety of arrangements. Harvey Probber, designer and manufacturer.

Sara Lobell, designer and manufacturer.

Cocheo Brothers, designers and manufacturers.

Sectional units shown in a corner arrangement. Most manufacturers produce a corner seat as an alternate to the table. Designer: Greta Magnusson Grossman, for Modern-Line.

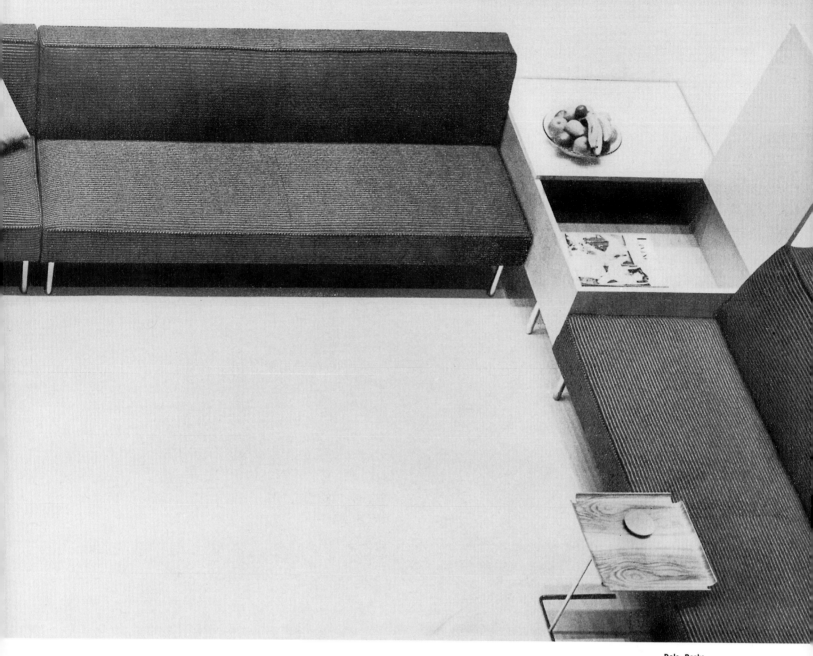

Dale Rooks

Modular furniture developed as a natural solution for the manufacturers' problem of standardization and the designers' problem of flexibility. Generally the use of the module has been confined to either cases or seating, but in this group various types have been combined. The corner tables (also storage units) occupy more than the corner so that the seats have adequate leg room. The group also includes an attached rear table and side tables (see page 163, top right). Construction is wood frame on metal legs, "No-Sag" springs, and foam rubber. Attached tables and storage units have plastic tops. Designer: George Nelson, for the Herman Miller Furniture Company.

designers

manufacturers and distributors

American Seating Company, 9th and Broadway, Grand Rapids, Michigan, 141

Arbuck Inc., 347 38 Street, Brooklyn, N. Y., 106, 130

The Arrow Upholstery Company, 119 West 24 Street, New York, N. Y., 150

Avard Inc., 66 West 55 Street, New York, N. Y., 137

Baker Furniture, Inc., Exhibitors Bldg., Grand Rapids, Mich., 98, 99, 100, 101

Baldwin Kingrey, 105 East Ohio Street, Chicago, Ill., 31, 65

Robert Barber Inc., 6 East 53 Street, New York, N. Y., 127, 151

The Bartos Company, 352 Butler Street, Brooklyn, N. Y., 17

Barwa Sales, 646 North Michigan Avenue, Chicago, Ill., 12, 124

P. & W. Blattman, Wädenswil, Switzerland, 139

Bonniers, 605 Madison Avenue, New York, N. Y., 21, 29, 31, 65

Carl Brorup, Blaagaardsgade 23, Copenhagen, Denmark, 31

Brown-Jordan, 146 West Bellevue Drive, Pasadena, Calif., 127

Cocheo Brothers, 1801 Willow Avenue, Weehawken, N. J., 165

Cramer Posture Chair Company, 1205 Charlotte Street, Kansas City, Mo., 129

Dunbar Furniture Corp. of Indiana, Berne, Indiana, 41, 62, 63, 73, 87, 93, 158, 161

Madress-Fabriken Dux, Malmo, Sweden, 93

Edgewood Furniture Company Inc., 208 East 27 Street, New York, N. Y. 32, 134, 136

Ficks-Reed, 424 Findlay Street, Cincinnati, Ohio, 134

Ron Fidler Associates, 203 South 8 Street, Columbia, Mo., 135

Fine Arts Furniture Company, Waters Building, Grand Rapids, Mich., 92

Finsven Inc., 870 Madison Avenue, New York, N. Y., 20, 21, 24, 36, 37, 41

Fulbright Industries, Fayetteville, Arkansas, 81

Gallo Original Iron Works Inc., 401 Park Avenue, Brooklyn, N. Y., 151

General American Transportation Company, 135 S. LaSalle Street, Chicago, Ill., 57

Gold Medal Folding Furniture Company, Racine, Wisconsin, 86

Allan Gould Designs, 166 Lexington Avenue, New York, N. Y., 41, 55, 72

Hansen, 978 First Avenue, New York, N. Y., 43, 71

Fritz Hansen, 3 Dronningsgade K, Copenhagen, Denmark, 43, 51

Johannes Hansen, Bredgade 65, Copenhagen, Denmark, 42, 43, 90

S. Hille and Company, Chigwell, Essex, England, 60

research: Suzanne Sekey

layout: Irving Harper and Suzanne Sekey George Nelson and Associates

book jacket: Irving Harper

printing: Guide-Kalkhoff-Burr, Inc.

binding: J. F. Tapley Company

engravings: City Photo Engraving Corporation